They Deserve a Second Chance

Shirley Alberta Roberts Combs

Shirley A. Combs
Prov. 3:5, 6

THEY DESERVE A SECOND CHANCE

Copyright © 1995

By

Shirley Alberta Roberts Combs

ISBN: 978-1-940609-13-3 Soft-cover

All rights reserved. Churches and other non-commercial interests may reproduce portions of this book without the express written permission of the author, provided that the text does not exceed five percent of the entire book.

This book was printed in the United States of America.

To order additional copies of this book, contact:

Shirley Combs
733 N.E. 18
Moore, Oklahoma 73160
By

FWB Publications

FWB

THEY DESERVE A SECOND CHANCE

Dedication

To my parents, Rev. William Thomas and Lucy Marie Roberts, for their loving example to their six children, our families and the many others who have been nurtured in their home.

To our three M.K.* children, Kemper, Cindy and Tania, who unselfishly shared their home and parents with our first street child, Marcos, and the many others who followed.

To the *Igreja Batista Livre* (Free Will Baptist Church) in Araras, Sao, Paulo, Brazil, and the staff and volunteers at *Lar Nova Vida* who provide a home of hope to street children.

Especially to my missionary husband, Jim, who took me to Brazil in 1964, walked the cobblestone streets with me, let me dream dreams for myself and others, and now helps me see them come true.

* Missionary Kid

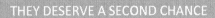
THEY DESERVE A SECOND CHANCE

A SECOND CHANCE: An Unforgettable Story of Rescuing Brazil's Street Children, by **Shirley Roberts Combs.**

THEY DESERVE A SECOND CHANCE

CONTENTS

Acknowledgments 7
Foreword 9
Preface 11

Part One:
WOUNDED lAMBS

Chapter 1—Counting Lambs by Five's 15
Chapter 2—Another Set of Five 27
Chapter 3—Our Little Wounded Lambs 41
Chapter 4—A Lamb Goes Astray 57
Chapter 5—Even a Child Is Known by His Doing 61
Chapter 6—The First Rescue 69
Chapter 7—A Second Chance 79
Chapter 8—A Call to Battle 85
Photo Section 90

Part Two:
MIRACLE STORIES

Chapter 9—The Beginning, Death Squads 105
Chapter 10—Like Walking on the Water 111
Chapter 11—When Have We Seen You without Shelter? 115
Chapter 12—Miracles That Lead to Faith 123
Chapter 13—When Have We Seen You Hungry? 129
Chapter 14—When Have We Seen You Naked? 135
Chapter 15—Money Doesn't Grow on ... What? 139
Chapter 16—To Judge Wisely 145
Chapter 17—Love and Acceptance 149
Chapter 18—The Guilty Bride Reveals Her Secret 155

THEY DESERVE A SECOND CHANCE

THEY DESERVE A SECOND CHANCE

Acknowledgments

If it had not been for the encouragement and requests of women from prayer retreats where I have shown my "miracle scroll" in West Virginia, Kentucky and especially Oklahoma, this book would have taken much longer to appear. The state president of the Oklahoma WNAC, Mary Alice Bridgeman, wept when she heard the Miracle Scroll stories and encouraged me to write them down. She was called into the presence of the Lord before this book was printed and her tears have now turned into everlasting joy.

One hundred legal size pages of handwritten manuscript survived a wreck Jim and 1 suffered during furlough, and from the insurance settlement he bought me a Laptop Notebook (computer). He allowed me to leave him driving in silence as I typed for hours and hours over the thousands of miles we traveled to meet our appointments in churches and schools from state to state.

A special thanks to furlough friends during my writing months. For example, Bonnie Williams helped me read my new book, *Word Perfect 6 for Dummies;* her husband, Pastor Jerry Williams, gave up his desk while we stayed with them during an area conference. And *obrigado* to fellow missionary friends, Ken and Marvis Eagleton, for their help in proofreading. Without the professional expertise and patience of Bill Stewart, I would not have reached my deadlines.

Our daughter, Tania, keeps a list in her computer of all the books she reads. It includes hundreds of titles! Undoubtedly, she has gained editorial skills over the years of reading, because she could almost "read my mind." She helped me arrange, in a more understandable way, this

THEY DESERVE A SECOND CHANCE

wonderful story of what God has done. Then, when furlough was drawing closer to the end and our conference schedules increased, a friend who shares my Oklahoma roots, Larry Hampton, stepped in and provided the professional editorial skills needed to prepare the story for printing.

Of all the people who have influenced the writing of this story, no one has helped more than our dear friend, Don Robirds. He and his wife, Carol, and their children were on the airplane with us on that December day in 1964 when we traveled together to the beautiful country of Brazil as newly appointed missionaries. He and his efficient editorial assistant, Tammy Strickland, donated literally days of labor as we worked together in their offices in Antioch, Tennessee. *Muito obrigado!*

The Rejoice Free Will Baptist Church in Owasso, Oklahoma, has encouraged me in this ministry and has given me full use of all their office machines and staff talents.

And in all my ways I acknowledge Him who has, since I gave Him my life at nine years of age, directed my paths ... especially down the streets where children are cold, hungry, scared, alone and desperately waiting for you and me to care.

THEY DESERVE A SECOND CHANCE

Foreword

Evidence of the powerful working of an omnipotent God permeates the pages of this book. Those reading this compilation of stories surrounding the dynamic rescue of Brazil's street children undoubtedly will have their faith strengthened.

Shirley Combs is one of the most compassionate missionary servants I know. Her commitment and dedication to reaching the "social undesirables" of Brazil radiate from the pages of this book.

I have known Shirley and her husband, Jim, since our days at Free Will Baptist Bible College in the late 1950s and early 1960s. My family traveled on the same plane with them when they first went to Brazil in 1964. We studied the Portuguese language together and worked closely with one another for several years.

In all of that time and since then, Jim and Shirley have labored faithfully for the Lord and He has blessed their ministry. Yet, God used them during their most recent missionary term in ways so marvelous as to seem incredible. Miraculous transformations brought rays of hope to many street children, orphans and even adults.

Every person who takes the time to soak up the life-changing accounts set forth by Shirley's writing will certainly be changed also. Who can read of the answered prayers of these simple children and doubt for one second that God cares about them? And who can witness the transformation of lives portrayed in this book without getting excited

THEY DESERVE A SECOND CHANCE

over God's working?

No other book which I have read in recent years has set forth such an abundance of incidents proving God's interest in children, simple things and simple people.

This is not a story just for Free Will Baptists or just about Free Will Baptists. But every Free Will Baptist should read this book! Each should sense deep satisfaction and godly pride over what is being done through these special servants sent out by Free Will Baptist Foreign Missions.

Each of us should bow in prayer expressing gratitude to God for what He is doing. Then we should ask Him what He desires from us who live in such abundance while so many are suffering and dying at the hands of Brazil's death squads.

It is sad indeed that many people see these destitute street children as "pests" needing to be exterminated. Shirley Combs and those in the Araras Free Wall Baptist Church see them as "wounded lambs" needing to be rescued. And, by God's grace, they are pulling many from the fire.

> Don Robirds
> *Director of*
> *Communications*
> *Free Will Baptist Foreign*
> *Missions*

Preface

Very few people know their names. Some see them as frail little bundles of skin and bones curled under a piece of cardboard in an alleyway, on sidewalks, under bridges or park benches with only the privacy of darkness to cover them.

Who are they? Where did they come from? Is it true they are being assassinated, shot down by society's "pest control"? The answers to these questions led us down paths we had never traveled before, nor had any other of our colleagues.

One of the Lord's disciples dared to step out and do something that none of the others ever did. When Jesus called for Peter to come to Him (Matthew 14:29), he climbed out of the ship and walked on the water to Jesus. Most remember that Peter, seeing the boisterous wind, began to sink (vs. 30). But he did walk on the water! When he cried to the Lord to save him and grasped Jesus' stretched forth hand, he walked on water back to the ship.

Peter may have learned a greater lesson and received a greater blessing because he was the one who walked on the water, but the incident encouraged the other disciples as well. As a result of this experience, they worshiped the Lord and declared that He was the Son of God. That is the reason for any miracle. Someone has said, "Miracles are not the foundation for the household of faith, but they are the path that leads to the door."

God opened the door for a small *Batista Livre* (Free Will Baptist) church in Araras, Sao Paulo, Brazil. He said, "Come." We saw no raft, no life jacket, no bridge. We never had a course in walking on water, defying the pull of gravity or rearranging the molecules in water to hold the weight of a human body. But the Lord said, "Come," and the only thing

THEY DESERVE A SECOND CHANCE

between us and His outstretched arm was water. Not gentle, smooth, peaceful water but a stormy, choppy, noisy sea of misery with a boisterous wind carrying the bodies of Brazil's street children.

This book is a collection of true stories* about some of the children we have taken in at *Lar Nova Vida* (New Life Children's Home) in Araras, Sao Paulo, Brazil, a city of 100,000 people. I have written the story from my vantage point as director of the Children's Home. I also relate a "success story" of a street child we took into our own home seven years before we opened the Children's Home. He is completing the cycle by helping other street children reach for the outstretched hand of Jesus. Only He can lead them through this stormy life. I also include the account of how the home was started. Finally, I relate an exciting collection of miraculous answers to prayer concerning the daily needs of the children.

*Some names have been changed to protect the identity of those involved.

THEY DESERVE A SECOND CHANCE

PART ONE
WOUNDED LAMBS

> THEY DESERVE A SECOND CHANCE

CHAPTER ONE

COUNTING LAMBS BY FIVE'S

"I'm going to kill every one of these brats if somebody doesn't help me with them!"

The threat came from a young woman surrounded by four small children, who looked to be between the ages of two and eight. As my eyes tried to assess the situation, I was impressed at how attractive the young woman appeared in her skimpy but modern clothes in contrast to the poorly clad children with shaven heads. Street children.

I looked up at the policewoman filling out papers at the counter of the women's police station. She shrugged her shoulders and then informed me that Dra. Anaraci was ready to see me.

During the entire time we were talking about another case, relating to a child at the New Life Children's Home, I kept thinking of those children hearing their mother's threat. After the chief of police finished her business with me, I asked her about the situation.

"Who, Iris? She has a thick file and we have been listening to her threats for years. She grew up in a reformatory, met her husband there, and they got married. They have five children. Her husband is in prison right now. She was reared in a state institution, so she thinks the government owes a living to her and her little brood."

"Would she really kill her kids?" I ventured.

"No, she likes them in her own strange way. As long, as she has them, she has guaranteed social

THEY DESERVE A SECOND CHANCE

help. So she won't be letting them get too far away. I just hope none of them ends up at your home or you will never be free of the trouble she can make for you. Folks say she takes drugs and gets a little crazy sometimes. Her kids beg in the streets."

When I left the police chief's office, I found Iris still in the waiting room with her children.

"Excuse me, *Dona Shirley.*" It surprised me that she knew my name.

"This lady here was telling me you operate the *Lar Nova Vida* (New Life Children's Home). How is little Zico doing? His mother is my neighbor."

"He is doing great! He is healthy and happy. How is his mother?"

She tugged at the hem of her miniskirt. "She's loaded today. I don't know how long she can last. Don't you want some more kids? They all know Zico."

I looked at her little ones and one started rubbing her hand down my skirt. "It looks like these children have a mother. A young, healthy one. No matter how simple your life may be, it is always better for children to stay together. There is no person better suited to care for children than a sincere, dedicated mother. Don't you agree?"

"I agree," she said under her breath.

Word had gotten around town about the Children's Home that had just opened for the street children of our city. We accepted children from birth to 12 years of age sent to us by the juvenile judge.

Quite some time after that encounter with Iris, after the number of children in our home passed 20, *we* heard she had contracted the AIDS virus. Then one day she paid me a visit at the home. She accompanied Zico's mother on the Saturday morning visitation day.

"They tell me I have AIDS, so I think they'll be taking my kids from me," she stated. "I asked them

THEY DESERVE A SECOND CHANCE

to let me keep little Eunice as long as I can. My oldest child, Angela, is 11. She can take care of herself. However, she is already begging me to let her come, too. She needs to work. I want to know if you can promise me something. Can you keep them from adopting out my kids until after I die? Can you find them Christian families if they leave the home?"

It would be difficult to make promises before I even received her children, but I doubted that a set of siblings would have a profile for adoption. Of course, I would want to find Christian homes for the children if I had any influence in the situation.

"Make sure you visit your children each Saturday if they are sent here. They will be going to church every Sunday, and we invite parents to sit with their children during the services. Iris, we must not just prepare for this life. Make your peace with God and you can be guaranteed that someday you and your children will be reunited. You will never need anything and you won't have to be separated. Jesus died to give you that hope, so accept Him as your Savior."

Iris was a practicing Spiritist and had sought solutions to her life's problems in the voodoo and black magic practiced in the slum area where she lived. Before her children were sent to the home, I visited her in the *corredor* of her *Vila*. It was a corridor with tiny rooms built on either side. Behind each rotting, wooden door lived five to ten people. She and her children lived in one of the rooms with a makeshift bed, a table and sacks of clothes begged for in the streets (or stolen off clothes lines). No water. No electricity. And about 50 people shared the same outside toilet and a water hose.

The day I visited her, she was screaming at Lucio, the youngest of her three sons. He had pricked himself with the syringe she used to take

THEY DESERVE A SECOND CHANCE

drugs, not a good thing for a mother with the AIDS virus to leave lying around. She called the name of one of her Spiritist idols, to whom the child had been dedicated, and hoped the boy would be protected.

In practically the same breath, she told me about a neighbor who needed prayer. She had suffered a stroke and lay paralyzed in her bed.

"Let's go pray for her," I suggested.

"Oh no, her husband is a beast and won't allow any of us near them."

She followed me to the door, however, and waited for me as I entered the dark room. As my eyes adjusted to the darkness, I saw a pale woman lying in the bed with a blanket over her. The stench just about knocked me over. It was then that I saw slop jars (cans, really) sitting around on the floor and molded food in plates on top of the stove. At least she had a stove. But no small propane tank rested beside it, a sign that it had probably been sold for booze.

"She can't talk," Iris called into the room.

The woman's curious eyes looked at me and then toward the door with a flicker of fear. "Hello, *senhora*. You don't know me, but I was visiting Iris and she told me you had a stroke. I have come here to help you." She shook her head in agreement but looked back at the door.

"Are you hungry?" I asked her.

She shook her head no.

"When did you last eat? Will your husband bring you something? First of all, let me tell you that I came in Jesus' name and I want to pray for you. May I pray for you?"

She shook her head yes.

I was so used to going into the *vila* and visiting these people that it didn't usually seem strange. But at that moment I realized that I was surrounded by some of the most notorious criminals of our region.

THEY DESERVE A SECOND CHANCE

Thieves. Drug pushers. Assassins. Homosexuals. Prostitutes. Hundreds of people of that one *vila* had AIDS. I knew half of them, and the other half knew me! Just which one of these criminals was this woman's husband, I didn't know. But I certainly wanted to get a few things done before he came back.

The first and most important was to show Jesus to this woman. She was the very type that Jesus spent time with. What an honor to represent Him at that precious moment by the woman's bedside.

After we finished the prayer, I opened my eyes to see a smile on the woman's face and tears glistening in her eyes. Next, to get rid of that stench!

How I wished for some gloves at that moment! But since I had none, I just started picking up the small cans used as slop jars, about six of them. I tried not to think about how long they had been sitting there. Since the dear woman could not get out of bed, I knew there must be other people in the house ... walking people. The neighbors told me she had two slightly retarded teen-age sons who were no help to her.

After I scraped out the molded food, Iris took the soiled pans from my hands and carried them to the water hose to wash. That left me free to start on the beds.

The two sons slept together on a twin-size bed. I soon discovered that they urinated in the bed. Okay, I could handle that. But when I started seeing little squiggling creatures crawling over the damp mattress, I have to admit, it was a first. Maggots. Maggots? Maggots!

I must have stood there frozen for a few seconds because when Iris called out to me, I jumped. *"Dona Shirley,"* she called. "Oh, please, leave now. Her husband is coming!"

THEY DESERVE A SECOND CHANCE

The curious neighbor women disappeared behind their rotten doors, except for Iris. She waited in the corridor.

The poor woman in the bed started making sounds from her throat and I went over to comfort her just as her husband came in the door.

"Good afternoon, *senhor,*" I greeted him. I felt I needed to control the conversation although he wasn't as large a man as I had imagined him to be.

"I came to pray with your wife and I think she was pleased. She must get very lonely here by herself and now she has been reminded that she has a loving Father who knows her name and her needs."

One of his sons walked up behind him and then entered the room.

"We thought your wife might appreciate a little help cleaning up the room. Iris had just offered to wash her blankets for her."

"No, I don't want anybody in here." He spoke for the first time. "They just come in here to steal everything I have."

"But, *senhor,* did you know there are maggots on the mattresses?"

He let out a ragged chuckle, "Oh, yeah? Well, when I get in bed with the wife, there'll be one more in there."

His wife was lying still with her eyes closed. For her sake I asked, "If I promise to bring you another mattress tonight, will you let me take this out and burn it? And one more thing, let Iris wash those blankets so they can dry before nighttime. I'll guarantee she will not steal them."

He just nodded his head yes and stepped aside for me to leave.

I went over to kiss the little woman and tears were in her eyes again. Now all I needed was to find a mattress somewhere.

THEY DESERVE A SECOND CHANCE

By nightfall I had found a new mattress and some blankets.

A policeman friend offered to deliver the mattress in his van. It made an impressive sight to see the van pull up in front of the *corredor* on a mission of mercy, and I didn't mind at all having a uniformed friend for an escort!

When I asked my escort if he knew these people, he replied, "At one time or another I have met them all, I guess. They aren't exactly the type of men I would expect to introduce you to, *senhora.*"

We both smiled as he carried the mattress into the little room. It was good to forget barriers of rich or poor, criminals or law officers, to be able to see one more crooked smile on my new friend's face as she watched strangers go in and out of her little prison. Somehow, I knew the Lord was smiling too.

Soon after that incident with Iris in the *corredor,* her children were sent to the home. First, three little boys—Lucio, Edgar and Timoteo—arrived. Later, little Eunice arrived, and then Angela. At first the boys fought, kicked walls, screamed and didn't want to cooperate. We knew that they were scared, suspicious and skeptical of our love. But love conquers, and it didn't take as long as we thought.

Soon, better times outnumbered the bad and they became loving, gentle little children. Then suddenly they would become defiant and seem to regress. We suspected some "spiritual" problems were still troubling them.

When children arrive at the home, we treat them immediately for lice, worms, skin disease and rotten teeth. We also take away their cigarettes and pacifiers. And just as certain, beyond the physical needs, a spiritual, supernatural disturbance usually lingers. Their families have offered many of them to demon spirits in rituals before they arrive

THEY DESERVE A SECOND CHANCE

at the home. Some types of spirits only leave with "prayer and fasting."

One Sunday night, the unperceived spirits of several seemed to descend at one time! A few of the children were ill, as were the volunteers for that weekend. I was staying with the sick ones as well as all of the smaller children, while the older ones went on to church.

As I was giving medicines to the sick ones and putting them down for the night, I heard a terrible commotion in the kitchen.

I ran to the kitchen and found one of the boy's naked, blasting water all over the kitchen with a garden hose from the back yard. It was already flooded.

Suddenly, a crashing noise and screams came from one of the boys' bedrooms. I ran from the kitchen to the bedroom. I found those tiny boys had turned over one of the bunk beds and had pulled all the clothes out of the shelves.

The sick ones started crying, and I was about to join in.

"Dear Lord, I am alone here. Please send a Christian to come and pray with me. I don't know which way to turn."

I sat down on the sofa, surrounded by noise from every direction. Then, above all the commotion, I faintly heard someone clapping at the gate (Brazilians clap instead of knocking at the door). A young man, his wife and their beautiful baby boy were there when I arrived.

"Vanderley, Marcia. Oh, thank God you both are here. You are an answer to prayer. Please come in."

They followed me up the stairs of the veranda and into the house. As we went from room to room, I explained to them what I had seen.

"Will you help me gather the children together so we can have prayer?"

THEY DESERVE A SECOND CHANCE

Soon the children were reluctantly seated around on the sofas and floor of the living room where they usually had family devotions. Suddenly, as we were talking, little Lucio—Iris' youngest son—started growling, *"Deus e mentira* (God is a lie). *Jesus nao existe* (Jesus doesn't exist). *Odeio aqui e quero escapar (I* hate it here and want to escape)."

"Oh, Vanderley, please pray right now!"

He prayed in the powerful name of Jesus and through His blood that any evil spirit controlling the child and others would leave immediately. The children started to calm down.

After the prayer, little Lucio meekly asked me, "Aunt Shirley, do you want me to sweep and help you clean up?"

Gone was the growling voice with its blasphemy, and in its place was the sweet little voice of our little five-year-old. He had come back and his tormentor had left.

On New Year's Day, Vanderley and his dear little baby boy were called to be with the Lord during a terrible motorcycle accident. Marcia was in the hospital, barely alive. They had been to a watch-night service at the church.

The largest crowd I had ever seen in the cemetery came for their funeral. Since January is summertime in Brazil, the sun was bearing down on our heads around the graveside. Many in the crowd remembered different things about Vanderley, a young man so full of smiles for everyone. I couldn't help remembering his being in the right place at the right time and claiming the blood of Christ in favor of our little ones.

With her five children taken care of, Iris decided she wouldn't live alone.

"Did you hear that Iris and Joe are together?" someone asked.

No I hadn't, but the next time she appeared at visitation, she told me! I asked, "Don't you think about the fact that you are still married?"

"My old man's in prison and I don't know for how long."

Most of her friends in the *vila* were not married and usually their children had different fathers. But all of Iris's children have the same father. Each time he got out of prison, he would return, they would fight and he would leave her— bruised and pregnant. He even visited our church with his children in between prison terms.

Iris continued, "I figure since I've got AIDS and Joe has AIDS, it is better for us to live together rather than contaminate others."

Joe was the brother of one of our little girls in the home. During one of his stays at the Spiritist sanitarium, attendants had discovered he had AIDS and contacted the authorities. I entered the picture after he was dismissed from the sanitarium. Officials asked me to be present with him and his mother when they were informed of his condition.

He was loose on the streets without being informed of his condition! It was my first case, so I went to authorities "suggesting" that they tell him quickly. He was a very active young man, 19 years of age, with regular fights, girlfriends and syringe partners. He worked in the cane fields with a machete and could get wounded and need medical assistance.

The psychiatrist handling the city's cases didn't have an opening until later in the month! I just had to live with the "secret" all those days and try not to think about all the lives which could possibly be contaminated during that time.

Now Iris was sitting in front of me, mixing her complicated life with his.

THEY DESERVE A SECOND CHANCE

"What about the possibility of having a child? Have you thought about that? This is no good at all, Iris. Please don't do this. Give your life to the Lord and be a good example to your children while you still have time with them."

"I can't make any more babies. I was fixed with the fifth one.

How wrong she was!

At one time she started losing weight because of her virus. Folks started commenting, "Have you seen how much better Iris is looking? Maybe she is going to be healed. Or maybe she's expecting a baby!"

She confessed to the house mother, *Dona Antonia,* that very fact one visitation day. She said she would just have to abort the child. Abortion is illegal in Brazil, which means she would be placing herself in the hands of people who use crude and unsanitary means of killing unborn infants.

Dona Antonia urged her, "You are not going to right anything with more wrongs. Have your baby and we will take care of it."

"Even if it has AIDS?"

"Of course, my dear. You must not kill this child."

She was four months pregnant but other pressures overwhelmed the motherly advice she had been given by the Christian housemother. So she aborted the child herself.

She and Joe even showed up together at our church to see her children and his sister. Our Sunday services remind me of the scripture that says we are debtors to both Greeks and barbarians. Our church is made up of middle-class professional people (representing the educated Greeks) who reach out to the community's most destitute (the illiterate barbarians).

In the Brazilian class-conscious society, it was

THEY DESERVE A SECOND CHANCE

a miracle they were together in the same building. How wonderful to be able to present a gospel that reaches the down-and-outer and the up-and-outer. When they accept God's redemptive plan, it brings them to the same level, into the same body.

It is a joy to see the spiritual growth of Iris' children and see their healthy outlook on life now. We wish we could say the same thing about Iris. We keep trying but she is so unpredictable!

One day she went to a local live radio talk show for people who have complaints about the city government (like potholes in the streets). She, however, complained about the Children's Home and told lies to the thousands of people listening in.

Soon, a reporter visited the home to investigate her claims. The house parents politely told him that the stories were not true and they had nothing else to say.

He immediately interviewed the neighbors living around the Children's Home. We later learned that the neighbors declared Iris' report to be false. To the contrary, they testified that they had never seen a family so united, happy, respectful and mannerly as what they were seeing from New Life Children's Home!

Iris' children are included in that report, for they have been given new life, a second chance.

THEY DESERVE A SECOND CHANCE

CHAPTER TWO

ANOTHER SET OF FIVE

How about five at a time? Our first encounter with them was a fleeting contact years before. Some church members passed by the house of a young woman and took her, her several children (including twin babies) and her nephew to Sunday school at the *Batista Livre* church in Araras. Years later, women from the church came to us with a sad, complicated story of the little nephew and his young brothers and sisters.

"They are hungry, always sick and not even in school," a relative began. "I have a house full of children and take care of my invalid mother. I check on them when I can and take things to them but it is so pitiful, I can't live with it anymore."

Another woman offered, "If we report them to the authorities, they'll take them and send them off somewhere and they'll get separated. There are six of them but one is old enough to take care of himself, and one, Danilo, works for his uncle in a bicycle shop. They see him every day and can keep an eye on him."

"How old are the other four," I asked, knowing that the story was going to be complicated.

"They are from two to nine years of age. The youngest are girls, Carina and Catarina, and the other two are Tadeu and Pedro. The boys are just loose in the streets and she can't handle them anymore. Oh, it's just so pitiful!"

"What about their parents?"

THEY DESERVE A SECOND CHANCE

They looked at each other, and their expressions indicated the strain they felt from admitting a good friend could be the source of such a story.

"Their mother is an alcoholic," the lady answered. "She used to be a nice looking girl and a hard worker, but now she is so sick she doesn't cook, wash clothes or clean the house. The kids stay out in the streets all day. She yells at them, they yell back at her, then they run out of her way."

"And her husband?"

Again they exchanged looks, "He left."

"How many fathers are involved?"

"Three different fathers, but the last one legally adopted the others. The last three are his. He doesn't live in town."

For some reason I wondered if this father knew the plight of his children.

By this time we were seated around the dining room table and my heart went out to these women.

"First of all, we only accept children sent to us by the juvenile judge. Our home is here so children won't have to be sent off in different directions and we try our best to keep siblings together. But second, as you can see, we have wall-to-wall kids and have already passed our limit."

"You were our last hope. What are we going to do now?" The relative twisted her empty market bag in her hands and then placed a hand over her mouth to keep back the sobs.

"Well, my dear, God is your only chance and, for some reason, He has sent you here. You go report the case to the judge and tell him I referred you to him. We will abide by his decision. Since I have a feeling what his decision will be, the housemother and I will go with you now to visit the family."

Five of us loaded into the car for the drive across town to the last street of a low-income

THEY DESERVE A SECOND CHANCE

government housing area. Hundreds of tiny houses, each with its own drama, had postage-stamp size front yards, but the street was full of children who should have been in school!

However, something was missing from the scene. Except for a few boys kicking a can, their substitute soccer ball, children were not running freely, riding bikes, playing or laughing—things every child has a right to do. Instead, they were sitting listlessly on the curbs, pushing their bare toes in the sand collected in the gutters. Some had their heads lying on their folded arms which were propped up on their knees.

As we pulled up to park along the inclining curb in front of one of the houses, ours was the only car in sight. Neighbors were already looking out their doors and mothers were moving quickly to snatch up their smallest ones, naked except for tiny, faded T-shirts.

The children on the curb watched suspiciously until they recognized one of the women in the car.

"Vai chamar sua mamae," she ordered, and followed the child into the house to call her mother. We lingered for a few minutes outside.

After hearing a few moments of muffled conversation drifting out through the broken windowpanes, we entered the house followed by two boys. We had to pass through the five feet by eight feet kitchen to get to where the women were talking. Dirty pans and dishes filled the tiny sink and others were stacked on the floor. Molded food stuck to pans on the four-burner stove. The only shelf in the kitchen lay empty except for a medicine bottle. Grime and soil darkened the stucco walls.

The rest of the house was no better. Soiled clothes had been removed from the sofa and piled on the floor to make room for us to sit. Two small girls sat on the floor. They looked to be about ages two

THEY DESERVE A SECOND CHANCE

and five. The older one, Carina, was searching through the baby's kinky, but sparse hair. She stole a shy, sideways glance at us and then returned to her searching. She had such a sweet, meek look in her eyes.

The baby's eyes were red. She looked like she was battling the flu and maybe had a touch of fever. Baby Catarina looked up at her mother and then ducked her head quietly as her sister continued the private hunt for stubborn lice.

One frameless, enlarged photo hung on the dirty stucco wall. A smiling face looked down on us resembling only slightly the heavier, angry woman speaking in controlled tones to her friend, "I send the boys off to school each morning, but they won't go. I can't control them. You'd think they would stay around here to help, but they don't. They are driving me crazy!"

As she rambled on, raising her voice with each sentence, the younger boy, Pedro, ducked his head. But the older, Tadeu, shook his head and defiantly stared out the broken window.

I could imagine the children's plight in their weak, undernourished state, trying to keep their own school uniforms clean, stay awake in class and do the required daily homework in all their sorrow and filth.

The women were trying to convince the mother that both she and the children needed some help.

"Well, the baby can't go out with that bad cold. I've got to doctor her."

Hopeful glances passed between her friends. As I reached over and touched the mother, she didn't draw away.

"Listen, Irene, we are not here to be a threat to you. We want to look after you and help you take care of your children. We are here in the name of Jesus. May we pray for you and your children?"

THEY DESERVE A SECOND CHANCE

She nodded her head in silence.

"Children, gather around," I motioned to them.

Catarina climbed up on the bench beside her mother and I pulled the beautiful little Carina onto my lap.

"I wonder if your baby sister has ever heard this little song:

> Only three little words,
> I have learned by heart,
> God is Love!
> Tra-la-la-la-la-la-la-la."

The boys came in closer and the mother wiped the baby's runny nose with her skirt tail. They all respectfully listened as I prayed to the One who was looking down on that little scene, knowing what He intended to do. I didn't know what the judge would decide, but I knew in my heart that somehow God was bringing me into this story for some reason. And I was right.

In a few days, the courthouse caseworker informed us by phone that the four children were on their way. Their mother, Irene, was admitted to the Spiritist sanitarium for alcoholism and we were to take care of her children temporarily until she recuperated.

We were used to "temporary" arrangements being long-term so we started preparing a place in our home of refuge for four more needy children.

The first thing we did, after embracing them and showing them around the home, was to provide a nice hot bath, with a special lice-killing shampoo (we didn't want the other 20 children getting infected). We washed their little bag of dirty, foul smelling clothes in disinfectant, labeled them and stored them away.

By the time they were scrubbed and dressed with fresh, clean clothes, a hot meal was waiting for

THEY DESERVE A SECOND CHANCE

them. The children were shy but ready to eat a good meal, except for baby Catarina. She was hot with fever.

I called one of our volunteer nurses from the church and explained the child's symptoms. Soon she was at the home, the bundled up child was in the arms of another volunteer and they were off to the pediatrician. How thankful we were to have friends in the medical field who believed in our work and treated all of the children free of charge.

They came back with the expected but sad news that the child had pneumonia. When they showed the prescription of 21 injections, two a day, everyone around groaned. Brazilian doctors don't give injections at their offices. This is the duty of the closest pharmacist.

"She is just skin and bones. How are they going to find a place for the needles?" a volunteer exclaimed.

"Twenty-one of them!" someone else said. "She just got here. She'll hate us for putting her through this."

Her brother walked in at that time: "She had to take 21 injections last year, too. She surely won't like it, and I certainly don't want to hold her while she is getting them."

Everyone looked at me. Suddenly they volunteered me to hold her while she took the shots.

She was so tiny, and it was pitiful, but we were convinced it could be a matter of life or death. The first day's shots were easier on me because she was so weak she hardly put up a fight. But as I started dressing her for our daily trips to the pharmacy, she would start whimpering and big tears would roll from her sunken eyes. At the pharmacy, her whimper turned to screams.

It was misery for the other children at the home to see her suffer and they would invent tales for her

THEY DESERVE A SECOND CHANCE

about going to the circus and parks and the ice-cream shop.

"No, we will not tell her lies about this. We'll help her through this and pray for her to get well just as we do for all of you."

Day after day, I carried little Catarina in my arms as we walked to get the needed medicine for her feverish body. I sang, whispered to her and prayed for her all the way down the cobblestone streets and back.

Did she wish for her *mamae?* Would she live to go to the nursery at our little church and grow to sing in the booster band? Would I ever see those little eyes sparkle with glee and feel her thin arms around my neck and her little peck on my cheek?

It was difficult on the professionals at the pharmacy, too. I noticed they traded off quite often giving the injections. But one day we noticed an improvement in the child. She was doing so well by the eighteenth shot that I hoped she had taken enough. But the doctor said she needed to finish the treatments. So, after the twenty-first shot, we had a party with a healthy little girl.

Yes, she soon was in church singing in the booster band, her eyes sparkling with glee, and by her little hugs and kisses I knew those 21 trips to the pharmacy would be replaced with many better memories. I was right, but not totally.

Tadeu and Pedro continued to be rebellious, pushing the smaller boys around. But they were enrolled in school, and their bodies were filling out with all the food and care they were receiving. Their brother, Danilo, would pass by, look around and tell their brothers how good they had it. He said he was staying with his uncle until his mother got out of the sanitarium.

Little by little, however, the boys made friends

THEY DESERVE A SECOND CHANCE

with folks from the church and their attitudes improved. Little Carina was in kindergarten and the baby was fine.

At this point, someone else entered the picture.

A man's voice was coming through on the telephone, "Is this *Lar Nova Vida?*"

"*Sim, Senhor,* it is New Life Children's Home."

"I just arrived in town because I heard that my children are in the reformatory. I really want to talk to you folks."

"We will be glad to talk to you, and you will be glad to find out that your children are not in a reformatory. We are a group of Christians who care for the needy children of our community. It is our goal to help the child's family so that he can be integrated back into his home whenever possible. Just come by so we can talk, but please be frank about your side of the story and your intentions regarding your family."

He agreed, and I gave him directions to the house. Soon, a nice-looking man came clapping at the gate. I had prepared the children to meet their dad. Pedro, Carina and Catarina seemed to be pleased, but Tadeu declared he wasn't his "real" dad and disappeared. When *Senhor Francisco* entered, the three children hugged their dad and we all sat on the veranda. *Senhor Franciso* asked about Tadeu and the boy stepped quickly from behind a door and joined our little group. He still sought to leave the impression that he was not interested.

Senhor Francisco bragged on each one's appearance and progress in school. After a while, the children entered the house, except for Tadeu, and the father told his story.

He and his wife were having trouble and she threatened to kill him if he didn't leave. He knew it was due to her drinking and they had tried time and time again to work things out but they couldn't.

THEY DESERVE A SECOND CHANCE

"I know it was wrong to leave my kids. My wife wasn't drinking at the time, and she had a job. The oldest boy also was working. She would lock me out of the house when I came home after working in the fields, and I had to find a place to stay. She wouldn't even give me my clothes.

"She said she would get along just fine without me, and I guess I hoped it would be true. I tried to get her to let me take the kids with me." He looked over at Tadeu. "The older ones said they didn't want to go, so I told her I would take the youngest three. She went into a rage and I felt I just couldn't take anymore.

"Things started happening in the neighborhood and rumors started circulating about me. I had no way to defend myself. Like I said, I shouldn't have left my kids, but I did. Now I have left my job in another city and have come here asking to get them back."

"The judge said he hopes to give them back to your wife when she recuperates," I said.

"That sounds good but she has recuperated before and gone right back to drinking. The kids can't take many more times."

He hung his head down.

"Tell me about your life together. Was there a time when you got along?" I asked.

"Oh yes, the first years were good. I adopted her kids and after a while ours started coming. But she started drinking and started changing. I'm not saying that you don't have a nice place here. I'm grateful for the care you have given my kids, but I want them back. I can't believe all this has happened."

"Okay, *Senhor Francisco,* let me ask you this. Would you be willing to try it again with your wife? Are you still legally married to her?"

"Yes, I am."

THEY DESERVE A SECOND CHANCE

"What if you talk to the judge and tell him what you have told me? Get a job and go to your little house and clean it up. Paint it so it will be sanitary for your kids. God wants to restore homes and reunite families and this would be one way to get your children back. We will just pray that after your wife gets out of the sanitarium and sees all of you together, she will be well and will want to give it a try. If she is willing, are you?"

He looked off and said nothing. Somehow I appreciated his silence at that moment.

"It would certainly take a miracle for her to change," he answered, "but I am willing to try. I want my kids."

Right there on the veranda of the home we prayed, as many others had before him. *Senhor Francisco* left, but he kept his word.

By the time Irene left the sanitarium, she was much better, hopeful and determined. She accepted the painted house and the return of her husband in silence for a while. Someone from the courthouse phoned one day and said the children would be leaving that day to return to their home. We had mixed emotions. Maybe the children knew more than we, for even though they were glad their mother and dad were waiting for them, they cried at having to leave their loving family in the New Life Children's Home.

We made regular visits to their home, and were encouraged at first. But hostility was openly demonstrated during later visits.

Right in front of the children the mother told their father that if he didn't leave, she would kill him. She had attacked him with a butcher knife the night before as he was sleeping. He said she was sneaking off to the neighbors and drinking. As they

THEY DESERVE A SECOND CHANCE

talked, the children huddled in the corners, out of sight.

Finally, *Senhor Francisco* went to the judge to ask for his children. He was working in the harvest fields and making little, but he wanted to return to his state of Bahia (a state north of us). His mother and family lived there and he could get a better job. He also had letters from his mother asking for a chance to help with the children. In Brazil, as in many countries, it is a very difficult decision to prefer the father over the mother.

When his request was rejected, Francisco tearfully left his address with the authorities and asked again for his children. That bus ride to Bahia must have been the saddest of journeys.

As their father had predicted, Irene's recuperation didn't last long and the children were suffering. Authorities called one day and informed me, "We are sending Irene's children back to you, only this time there will be five. Danilo is coming too."

It had been a year since they left the home. The children were not in school, they were frail and had lost weight. The boys were smoking and experimenting with drugs and their rebellious spirit had returned.

But when they arrived at the gate, they were met with open arms and, once again, we began a program of acceptance, firm love, and prayer, prayer and more prayer.

Somehow their father heard they had returned to the home, so he began to send them cards and letters. He didn't stop with the children. He also sent letters and made phone calls to the Department of Human Services. He wrote me asking that I inform the judge of his continuing desire to

THEY DESERVE A SECOND CHANCE

care for his children. I made copies of his letters to me and to his children, along with my own reports, and took them personally to the judge.

Since it involved another state and another set of caseworkers and judges, the wheels of justice moved slowly. We still worked with Irene and found jobs for her which she would take and lose frequently. She was urged to visit her children on Saturday visitation days and another day according to her schedule, but she seldom appeared.

In the meantime, we had contact with Tadeu's biological father and he visited the home. He had recently been saved and was attending a Baptist church. His wife was with him and he said the Lord had convicted him about his duty toward his son. Tadeu had been saved and baptized. He and his brother, Danilo, were leaders in Bible memorization and personal growth in the church's Boys' Club. It seemed like a good time to discover a Christian father.

We suggested that his father visit him, become reacquainted and formally advise the judge of his desire to adopt and care for his son. It was encouraging to see a good relationship between the boy and his new family. After many months of prayerfully wading through bureaucratic red tape, notice finally came that Tadeu was going with his dad.

Then, finally, notice came that Pedro, Carina and Catarina's dad was on the way to pick up his kids. We packed clothes, toys, school supplies and blankets to send with our precious little ones, but they were taking in their hearts the most precious treasure. They knew Jesus was their Friend and that they had a loving, Heavenly Father taking care of them. Now, they also had a happy, earthly father somewhere on a Brazilian bus ... coming to get his kids!

THEY DESERVE A SECOND CHANCE

That left 12-year-old Danilo. We contacted his biological father, and the man said he would talk it over with his present family, but we never heard any more from him.

Danilo still works at his uncle's bicycle shop and goes to school. And he still has his family at New Life Children's Home, the *Batista Livre* church and a loving Heavenly Father who promises not to leave His children orphans.

THEY DESERVE A SECOND CHANCE

> THEY DESERVE A SECOND CHANCE

CHAPTER THREE

OUR LITTLE WOUNDED LAMBS

Some of our little ones have arrived at the home with physical problems.

Once, I was at the courthouse and had just left the judge's office when I was called back. A handsome young man, around 25 years of age, stood as I entered.

"Dona Shirley, this young man has come to me with a problem that perhaps you can help him with."

He didn't look like the usual father whose child ends up at the home. The judge continued, "The mother of his child left their year-old baby on his doorstep. She lives in a neighboring city and has been caring for him by herself until now. This young man lives with nine more men and he works. He can't take care of the baby, so he needs a place to leave him until he can arrange a place to live and get a baby-sitter."

After asking the man and the judge a few questions, I agreed to help with the child. I explained that we give the children Christian training and asked if he had any problems with our taking him to our church. He didn't.

"We'll do all we can to help him and we will expect you to visit him on Saturdays." "I work on Saturdays," He answered apologetically.

"Then we'll expect you on Sundays. You'll need to get acquainted with your son."

The caseworker and I went by to pick up the baby, Miguel, and discovered one thing the father and the judge had failed to tell us. The little boy

THEY DESERVE A SECOND CHANCE

was paralyzed on his right side: He couldn't sit up, crawl or talk, but his beautiful smile won our hearts. So off we went to present our little wounded lamb to the family.

A physical therapist from our church treated him without charge at a clinic and told us what to do for him at home. Time passed. Nestle company employees donated a special buggy for invalid children, and Miguel learned to sit up in it. Finally, he learned to sit in a high chair. Under the loving supervision of about 20 more children, little Miguel learned to feed himself with his one good hand and learned to form a few words.

About a year later, Miguel's father arranged for the boy's grandmother in Bahia to care for him. He learned and progressed while he was in our care, but we learned so much more from him as he lay stiffly on his little back month after month spreading sunshine in our hearts.

One afternoon I received a phone call from someone at the hospital. "We need a place to care for a child we have had in the hospital for a month. Would you have room in your Children's Home?"

"We only receive children sent by the judge," I replied. I certainly hated to tell anyone that we had already passed our limit.

"We are getting ready to call him," the caller responded.

"Why has the child been in the hospital so long? How old is the child? Is it a boy or girl?" I had a feeling I would be needing the information in order to give her an answer.

"The child is a four-year-old girl. When Fabiana came to the hospital she could not sit up, but she is improving. We have kept her a month but she really doesn't need hospital care any longer and

THEY DESERVE A SECOND CHANCE

we can't send her home. Her mother doesn't know how to care for her and we are trying to contact the father."

"In your opinion, would we need a nurse or professional help on a daily basis?"

She hesitated a moment and said, "Yes, I would say it would be a time-consuming job to care for her."

"We are past our limit on children and depend on volunteers to help," I answered. "We have no professional help on a daily basis. But let us know if you don't find anyone and maybe we can find someone at the church to care for her on a temporary basis."

Just a few minutes later the phone rang again. It was a person from the courthouse.

"We must ask you to keep this child. The hospital said you don't have any vacancies."

"That's true, but she also said Fabiana would need constant professional care and we don't have anyone on our staff available for that."

"The hospital can't take care of her anymore. Are you saying that you will not take her?" the court representative questioned.

"We have never refused to take any child the judge has sent," I said. "I have just answered your questions honestly"

In a few minutes they called back. The judge had overruled me and soon I was so glad he did!

Little Fabiana had beautiful eyes and a shy smile. The rest of her little body looked like a skeleton. What a challenge!

At first, she scooted around on her little bottom, but the other children treated her like a little doll. And soon she was a walking doll! What a miracle to see a four-year-old squeal in glee over her first steps amidst the applause of our household. How

THEY DESERVE A SECOND CHANCE

good God is!

During this time her mother and father were visiting her each Saturday. Her father played with her, put on her sandals and brushed her hair. He was so proud of her progress and wanted to take care of her. Her mother, however, sat watching them complacently, not participating in her care.

One visitation day they didn't show up. We heard on the news that Fabiana's father had been killed—shot five times in the back. The mother visited a few times after that, and then disappeared.

Our little wounded lamb was not alone, however, for God had sent her to our fold of refuge.

Another little wounded lamb brought to our "fold" was deaf and mute. Eight-year-old Roberto was sent to the home along with his two-year-old sister, Bimba. The other children and shy little Bimba were so good to help Roberto join in the family life.

He and his little sister enjoyed the church services, and we would almost forget that he lived in his own silent world.

He smiled easily and was always ready to make a funny face, but Bimba was always solemn. We couldn't know what memories were still locked inside her little mind. The first time I saw her smile, however, was in Sunday school while she was in the booster band choir. We were filming them that morning and captured her first smile—singing about the Good Shepherd.

One amazing part of their story hit me when I discovered their father was the one whom folks say shot Fabiana's father in the back.

Now the three children live together in peace and love as brother and sisters. The Gentle Shepherd carries the wounded in His arms.

THEY DESERVE A SECOND CHANCE

One little lamb had to be carried into the home because he couldn't walk. The authorities had recorded his age as about 11 months because of his size and development. We later found out that he was closer to 15 months of age.

Pus was running out one ear and down on his clothes, and suspicious sores were all over his body. We tried not to let him notice that we had to hold our breath while he was being bathed. The stench from his sores was so strong. Mateus' little body was about normal from the waist up, but his legs were the size of a child half his age.

Neighbors reported he had been left alone in a one-room house with a sister only three years of age to be his nanny. The mother had a drinking problem and had different men friends visiting at night. After investigations, Mateus was brought to our home. We always wondered why the three-year-old, Marina, was not sent to us.

Several months later, the police brought to our home two little sisters, Cida and Pamela. They were in the streets because their alcoholic mother had been sent away from the brothel where they had been living. They were Mateus' cousins and had been living in the same house with him.

Mateus was a favorite at the church and was passed around from one person to another. Soon, he gained strength in his legs and learned to take his first steps. Some things he needed to unlearn, too!

He, Cida and Pamela had many memories to erase and habits to break—adult-size habits! These three preschool children required constant vigilance because they would strip off their clothes and take other children under covers or into hidden corners and give "favors" and ask for "favors." More "birds and bees" scenes were humming around in

THEY DESERVE A SECOND CHANCE

these children's heads than I would have ever thought possible for even our older ones. These little lambs were street wise and left us older sheep blushing!

One day we received an unexpected call from the courthouse advising us that Mateus' mother would be picking him up in 30 minutes!

"He's going back to the brothel?" we asked. "We have been visiting his mother. I know she is now living with just one man, and her drinking problem seems to be better, but she doesn't even come to see the child on visitation day. She never calls him or asks about him. How long have you known about this order? Thirty minutes isn't very long to prepare his things and to prepare us for his leaving!"

In 30 minutes his mother was there.

We drove her and Mateus, along with a bag of things for him, a baby bed and a mattress to the house. Her "friend" was there and assured us that he agreed to care for the child. His sister, Marina, hid behind a door. Several other women were there holding babies. One asked me if I would take her newborn so that she could care for her other children.

Although I wished the best for Mateus, and was glad he was back with his mother, my heart was heavy.

Months went by and we visited him occasionally. He lost his glow (maybe it was covered up by the filth) and his smile. I wondered what scenes he was observing now that he was older.

Over a year later, we received another call from someone at the courthouse. "We are sending Mateus back to you along with his six-year-old sister, Marina. Their mother is in pitiful shape."

We were having a birthday party that day for the five children born in November. Mateus and

THEY DESERVE A SECOND CHANCE

Marina's two cousins were progressing in school and becoming sweet little ladies. It was a perfect way to celebrate the return of our little lost lamb, along with his sister!

How much does a two-year-old remember of his mother trying to commit suicide with him in her arms?

Jair was brought to us, along with his medicine for seizures, baby bottles and a few clothes. His young mother had tried to commit suicide several times but when she jumped in front of a car with Jair in her arms, relatives and neighbors insisted that authorities guarantee the child's security. Her other small son had already been adopted by a relative and since she took wonderful care of Jair, everyone was satisfied to let her keep him, until the last suicide attempt.

She was a petite, attractive woman and seemed dedicated to her small son. When serious emotional problems started to surface, relatives from both sides of the family wanted to care for Jair, including his father who was living with his sister.

Jair's mother visited her little boy regularly on visitation days and sometimes she would show up during the week to bring him something special. We would talk with her about the Lord's love and interest in her and in a solution for her family. She was going to a psychiatrist, a required therapy for regaining custody of her son. She showed us her medicines and talked about her life and family.

One Tuesday she showed up wanting to do volunteer work around the home. Jair was taking his afternoon nap. I perceived she needed to talk and since I needed the help, we worked at the scrub board together (that was before we got a washing machine) and then in the kitchen. She seemed in good spirits and before she left she told us good-bye and kissed her baby. Everything seemed normal.

The next evening one of her neighbor's called our house asking to talk to my husband, Jim. "Pastor Jim, Jair's mother told me once that if anything happened to her I should call you."

"What has happened?"

"I really don't know, but she came and told me she was going on a wonderful trip and wanted to tell me good-bye. She said she was going to her father's house who really loved her. She seemed calm and peaceful. I found out that she did the same to all the other neighbors.

"Nobody answers at her house and it is all locked up. Can you please come over? She said to call you if anything happened. Oh, I just have a feeling it has."

"I'll be right there." He left immediately and drove directly to the neighbor's house. She told him the story again. He tried calling and then pounding on the door, but he did not get an answer.

He called the police and they arrived quickly.

They broke open the door to her house and found her stretched across the bed. The police thought she was sleeping but Jim suspected an overdose attempt.

"Help me carry her to my car and I will rush her to the hospital."

"No, Pastor, we have called the ambulance and they should be here shortly."

"But there may not be time. Please, let me take her."

The police would not agree, so they all waited. The ambulance arrived and took her to the hospital. She was still alive upon arrival and they tried through the following day to save her, but it was too late. Her body and will were too weak to survive.

They had the wake at her house that night, but

THEY DESERVE A SECOND CHANCE

there was no priest. I was among the first to arrive so I put a little makeup on her face and painted her nails. It is a Brazilian law that the body be buried within 24 hours of death. They don't embalm the corpse, so flowers cover the body to keep down the smell of death. A veil is placed over the body to protect it from the flies.

Family members from both sides were there, including Jair's father. They looked around her house, so neat and clean, and picked up her little boy's toys and shoes and cried. So did I.

Since the red tape was slow to unravel, they needed a neutral place to leave the child until something was settled. Jair's father and his mother's sister visited him regularly, but they never wanted to visit at the same time.

Weeks turned into months. I talked with authorities about this dear little wounded lamb. His profile was different than all the other children. He had a family. They wanted to care for him and give him a home and individual attention, which he needed.

Very carefully I visited interested relatives on both sides of the family. Then I advised them to agree on someone among themselves to take care of Jair. Then they could express that agreement to the judge so the child could soon be with his family. It was hard to believe they were so reluctant at first.

I believed details on visitation and responsibilities could be worked out after Jair was back with someone in the family. If not, Jair would pass one more birthday in the home, but I felt sure it would be much better if he could be with his family.

When the day arrived for him to leave, it was harder for us than we had imagined. But Jair was healthier than when he came to us. He had been in a Christian home and had attended church for the

THEY DESERVE A SECOND CHANCE

first time in his life. The past had been replaced by many positive experiences. Now, if he still has memories of his young, beautiful mother, perhaps they will be the good ones.

Other little lambs also found their way into our home and into our hearts. Armando, along with five other brothers and sisters, was taken from his mother after a phone call to authorities. Most of the children were sent out of town, but his younger brother was adopted by local people. Armando was chosen by another local couple as a foster child. He was a beautiful child and very loving, but also very hyper. It was sometimes difficult to understand him.

He had been with his new family several months when the mother had a miscarriage, the father lost his job and they were very frustrated with Armando. He was not responding to their care and the school said he was impossible to control.

They tearfully returned him to the judge before their year's trial time was up. The judge sent him to us.

Under our care we saw him improve. His stuttering decreased and he lisped less frequently. He could go many nights without wetting the bed and could sit fairly still at kindergarten.

During this time, a lawyer at the courthouse met Armando and thought he would be ideal for her sister who lived in another state. The lawyer's sister traveled to Araras and began visiting Armando. They seemed to be compatible so she was granted permission to keep him during the next school vacation.

We received phone calls from them and Armando was having a great time—learning to ride a horse. The woman was very interested in a more permanent situation after school vacation. She was

THEY DESERVE A SECOND CHANCE

bringing him back to town to talk to the judge.

When they returned, the child brought back many more things than he had taken. The woman was quiet. Serious.

She related, "Everything was fine and he was getting along well with our little daughter. But he started acting strangely. He took a pair of scissors and cut up several tennis shoes under the bed. He set fire in the house. He suddenly wouldn't obey.

"We are going to leave him with you again and talk this over some more as a family. I am truly sorry."

Our little wounded lamb had been returned for the second time. He settled back into the family routine and didn't talk anymore about horses or trips.

Early one morning the court informed us that another couple was coming to the home to see Armando. They came in with a small boy and were introduced to Armando. He and the smaller child started playing together in the veranda and I talked to the couple.

I kept watching their little boy.

They explained, "We adopted our first child and thought it was time to adopt a brother for him. We aren't sure if the second child should be older or younger, but have decided to meet Armando."

Something was forming in the back of my mind and when I started asking them questions about their adopted child, they shifted on their benches and looked at each other.

The husband confided, "This must be strictly confidential, for the safety of our son is at stake. Yes, you are right. Now that we see them together, they do almost look like twins. You see, our son is Armando's brother. Since we were on the list at the courthouse for another child, they suggested we meet him.

THEY DESERVE A SECOND CHANCE

Armando gleefully agreed to go home with them and they made a nice-looking group as they left in their car that Friday night to return before church on Sunday.

Early the next morning they were back. I was curious about their early return.

"How did the visit go?" I inquired.

"We almost returned him last night. He started talking about not wanting another family. He wanted to go with his mother and father and he was sure they would be looking for him.

"Armando asked to return here last night, but we were hoping it would be better today. We must not allow his family to know where we live so they won't find out about the other boy. We are really sorry and disappointed."

Our little lamb had been returned for the third time!

He never asked for his family when he was with us in the home but when he got away he just would not cooperate. For such a tiny five-year-old, he really caused big problems.

A complicated chapter started unfolding for Armando with the visit of a woman and her two children. She was there to ask us to care for her two preschool children for a few weeks. While she was talking, the other children of the home were walking back and forth and invited her children to play with them. Suddenly she exclaimed, "Little boy, is your name Armando? Is it possible that you are Armando? Come here and let me see."

He walked up shyly to her and then looked over at me. I offered, "Sim, his name is Armando. Do you know him?"

"He is my grandson; my son is his father. We didn't know where they had taken him. Look at me, child. You remember me, don't you?"

She pulled him onto her lap and he smiled.

THEY DESERVE A SECOND CHANCE

As she started to leave with her children, I informed her that we had visitation on Saturdays for relatives of the children.

She said she would be back. When she returned, she had her son with her. There was no denying that Armando was his son. They looked so much alike. He was very charming and nice looking. The child clung to him during the whole visit.

He told us he had left Armando's mother and was living with another woman. The day the officials took Armando and their other children away, one son was with his dad. Later, he gave that boy back to his wife, Armando's mother.

In the meantime he had a tiny baby by the woman with whom he was living. On top of that, her 14-year-old daughter was now pregnant by him!

In the next weeks, his father returned several times. One time he had his mistress (or mother-in-law) with him. Another time he brought her daughter (mistress number two and stepdaughter), and at times he brought his other son. Confusing? Believe it or not, Armando greatly improved at home and at school during that time.

Then one day a woman clapped at the gate. "I'm looking for my son, Armando. My husband just told me he is here and I really want to see him. I had no idea where he was."

We called him in and, wow, what a reunion. She was a live-in maid and companion to an elderly lady so she told him she could not take him just yet. She began visiting him faithfully each week, but her husband didn't come back. After a year of legal red tape and many sessions of counseling with her, she was granted temporary custody of her son.

THEY DESERVE A SECOND CHANCE

The boy's father disappeared until about a year later when he and the young girl, who had his child, came by wanting to give us two babies! We said no, and we haven't seen him since.

Armando and his mother live in a tiny room with the bare necessities and I wish them well. We just pray that this time our little lamb will not be returned.

Others have come, and will continue to come, like Edson who was found begging in the street with a little lame arm. He had been badly burned and his body had been left to heal at random. Now he had lost some of his muscle control. There is Nelo, who had a mental block after helping his mother throw a murdered man into a river. And Miriam, who was found under a bridge crying and scared. Her father beat her mother to death and her brother was dying of AIDS.

Sometimes God surprises us with the beauty He can make from broken pieces.

The phone rang at the home one day: *"Dona Shirley, this is the health department calling. We have a newborn girl whose mother has died of AIDS at 19 years of age. We are checking the baby for the AIDS virus and we need to know if you would accept her if she proves positive—if she were sent to you."*

"I feel that I know the answer but let me check with the staff who would be dealing directly with her," I responded.

We had a conference with the workers and volunteers about the subject. It was a short meeting because all agreed to receive the child, even though it would be our first case of this type. I advised the health department of our decision and waited for their call.

About a year later, we received a visit from the

THEY DESERVE A SECOND CHANCE

child's maternal grandmother. This was her story:

"Since my daughter's death, I have been trying to take care of my grandbaby, Katia, and still hold down my job. Now my 14-year-old daughter is pregnant and will soon have her baby. I'm asking for help. Today, I went to talk with the authorities about placing Katia temporarily with your home. I know you take good care of your children. I can't stand to think of her being adopted out because I would never be able to see her again and the child would never know me as her grandmother." She broke down and cried.

When Katia came to us, she was a tiny little thing but adjusted quite well. Her test was not positive, but she had to be checked regularly because of her age. We discovered that her father also had AIDS.

In God's providence, a young Christian couple met Katia while visiting the Children's Home one day and began asking questions about adoption. We advised her grandmother, who visited her regularly, of the couple's interest in adopting Kdtia. We wanted to get her opinion. Katia was with us on a temporary basis (it had already been months, however). But we knew if the baby were in the grandmother's custody instead of ours, less red tape and confusion would exist since the grandmother could talk to authorities.

"They are willing to allow you to be a grandmother to her," I told the woman. "You can visit her whenever you like and they will tell her the truth about her adoption. They are Christians and will provide her with a good home and more individual attention than we can give her here. Since you feel you can't be a mother to her, this will give you a chance to be a grandmother. Think about it. We will pray that you will make the right choice."

She chose to meet the couple and when she saw

THEY DESERVE A SECOND CHANCE

the three of them together, she decided to allow them to adopt her grandbaby.

The couple adopted Katia knowing she could develop the AIDS virus. At two, she was wearing glasses and they continue to check her quite often for any other problems. But meanwhile, they are loving her and taking her regularly to see her grandmother!

THEY DESERVE A SECOND CHANCE

CHAPTER FOUR
A LAMB GOES ASTRAY

When the person chasing you with a butcher knife is your mother, to whom do you run?

This was nine-year-old Marta's dilemma. A neighbor saw the danger Marta was in as she was fleeing from her alcoholic mother. He put her on a public bus and told the driver to take her to safety. The driver let her out a few kilometers up the road in our city of 100,000 people. The streets represented distance from her mother, but certainly not safety. She didn't know anybody. She asked for directions to the women's police station, but when she arrived, the gate was closed for it was after 5 p.m.

Scared and hungry, she wandered through the streets, too shy to ask for help but dreading the soon coming darkness. Somehow she ended up at a home for the elderly, but the private owner had no facilities for children. At that time the Children's Home did not exist, but the man from the other home called a young man from our church who was serving on the committee to plan a future home for children.

When they called my home and told her story, we had a feeling the "future" plans were already materializing in a present need. We talked to our own children and they agreed to make room for another child temporarily. We had a two-bedroom home and five of us were living there at the time. We had just been given a little boy the day before.

It was June, wintertime in Brazil. The next month would be time for our first youth camp at

THEY DESERVE A SECOND CHANCE

Camp Evangelandia, in Jaboticabal, Sao Paulo. It provided a great place of loving rehabilitation and spiritual teaching for our new little lost lambs and for the many who came after them.

Marta showed signs of being a bright girl, and she could memorize well. But she could not read or write. She may have been the tallest girl in the first grade, but she was proud of her new uniform, shoes, book bag and supplies when we took her to her first day of school.

Over the years, as we have taken child after child to the public schools, teachers and directors have been very helpful. They are grateful to have someone assisting with the great problem of street children. Little Marta probably helped form their good opinion.

Every child has a right to an education and Marta didn't disappoint us when we gave her that chance. At church, she would be the one chosen to present poetry, narrate a program or perform in a play. At the end of the school year, she was the top student in her class!

Of all the children in the Children's Home, she seemed to be the most sensitive to spiritual things. She was the first girl at the home to accept Christ, then she was baptized with others. She was helpful and obedient and showed fruits of spiritual growth. And she was loyal. But that loyalty got her into a lot of trouble. She was more timid and quiet than the older girls who came into the home. They would threaten her with, "You can't be our friend anymore," and convince her to go along with some of their pranks and ideas.

Once after school she left with two older girls who wanted to visit their old slum area. When they decided to hitchhike to the capital city of Sao Paulo, she refused to go. We found her sitting in the dark room of a shack and she said she was just praying

THEY DESERVE A SECOND CHANCE

that we would find her. After returning to the home, the other two girls related some horrifying experiences of their trip. We hoped they all had learned their lesson—especially Marta.

Somehow rejection by her own mother and the loss of her father when she was very young planted in Marta a yearning to belong, to be accepted. She was having a rough time of choosing the right people to give her that security.

Along with her public schooling, we sent her to special classes for crochet, knitting, textile painting and artistic greeting card craft work. She was diligent in everything she tried.

The family of the local church pastor gave special attention to Marta and helped her feel more secure. Our first little lost lamb was a good example of a success story.

But the wolf was close by. In attempts to relieve our crowded situation at the home, the judge ruled that all our girls would be taken out and given to some nuns who wanted to open an orphanage for girls. We did not want to accept this ruling.

During this time, one of our oldest girls got upset and decided to run away. She and another of her home sisters invited Marta to go with them. All their lives they had run to the streets when trouble came, but hardly ever by themselves. Marta was torn between her love for the only home she had known for over three years, and her loyalty to the sisters she longed for but never had. She decided to run.

The judge ultimately overturned his ruling and we were able to keep our girls, but these three were already gone.

When they finally called and asked for someone to get them, they had been sleeping under a bridge in a city of 15 million people. It was not what they wanted.

THEY DESERVE A SECOND CHANCE

But it was too late. We were told we could not go after them and if they returned, they could no longer live at the Children's Home. The longer they waited for someone to get them, the more rebellious they became. Weeks later they arrived at the bus station in town and called the vice president of the home, Isabel. She had to take them to the judge and he gave them over to the nuns.

Marta had left an obedient little lady and returned weeks later very bitter and hurt. She commented to church people visiting her that she wanted to return to her family at New Life Children's Home. She threatened to break every statue she could see if they made her worship idols where they took her! Our little lamb was upset.

May this little lamb always remember that her Good Shepherd is forever nearby and will never lead her astray.

CHAPTER FIVE
EVEN A CHILD IS KNOWN BY HIS DOING

Can a small child be used by the enemy and filled with an evil spirit? Well, let me ask you this: Can a small child be saved, filled with the Holy Spirit and used by God?

At the very beginning of our ministry with the street children we began family devotions at night. Once while I was praying with them I had a strange feeling and I opened my eyes as I continued praying. One nine-year-old girl was stopping up her ears with her fingers, gritting her teeth and staring straight at me. The other children had their eyes closed.

Immediately, I began praying in the name of Jesus and through His precious blood and then I started singing in Portuguese, "There is Power in the Blood!" The other children opened their eyes and joined in the singing.

The girl's mother told us that she had offered her daughter to a Spiritist god when she was a baby. Many times we talked and prayed with the girl and she was transformed for a time. She had been a gang leader of children and had been sniffing glue and was known for using a pacifier when she asked for things in the street. It is common for older children to use pacifiers in Brazil. At one time, the schools had to pass a rule that all students must keep their pacifiers in their lunch boxes and they could only be taken out at recess!

But at the home, the girl had to give up her pacifier and cigarettes. She was enrolled in school,

THEY DESERVE A SECOND CHANCE

attended church and during her years with us she turned into an attractive young lady.

She still had her bad days however, even though she said that she accepted Christ, she didn't show much spiritual fruit. Not only would she run away, but she would take the younger ones with her and they would follow her as though she were the Pied Piper. She hitchhiked to other cities and taught the other younger girls how to handle themselves around the truck drivers!

She advised the other girls that if they were reprimanded for something, just invent a lie about some man's behavior toward them and people would back off. At times she was a 12year-old giggling child, playing dolls with the younger girls; then, suddenly she played the role of gang leader and wanted to go to the streets.

One Wednesday night, she slipped out of church with two of the younger girls and ran away. The judge said to let her alone and he would settle the problem. The other two girls returned but she had disappeared.

A letter from the judge arrived asking me to have her at his office on a certain day. Nobody knew where she was, but I noticed that the day scheduled to see the judge happened to be her birthday. I went to talk to her old neighbors and told them I was going to make her a birthday cake. Then I would take her to see the judge. I hoped the neighborhood grapevine would get word to her wherever she was hiding. I wrote a time on a piece of paper and gave it to them, but they said they couldn't read. I drew a clock showing the time and left some money for a telephone call.

Lunch was ready and the cake was baked so I passed by her house, a makeshift room with no water or electricity. Happily she was there waiting on me. My heart ached during lunch and even

THEY DESERVE A SECOND CHANCE

during the happy moments when she blew out the candles-13 of them. She had lived in our own home and then in the Children's Home, but somehow she had not allowed God to cleanse her of the tormentors inside her.

After the judge gave her a stern lecture, he told me I would no longer be her guardian. I was required to return her to her mother's hut. Soon she was back on the streets from which she came. I left her with an invitation to visit our home and to be sure to attend church. She did both for a while.

Now, at times, she is a beautiful teenager and at other times you can see her in the streets, dirty, barefoot and sucking on a pacifier, surrounded by other dirty, hollow-eyed children. I hear reports that she has been caught stealing from local merchants, but when taken to the police, she is released because she is a minor.

The girl is a minor now, but who knows if she will live to be an adult. The mother who had offered her daughter to the idol has died from drink and drunkenness. The mother had said she had offered her to the god symbolized by a certain bird, a god of sex and passion. The god was to give great success, health and power. A promise by the Father of Lies. The girl has now been diagnosed with tuberculosis and the AIDS virus.

In spite of it all, I will never, never give up on this dear one. She is a wounded, runaway lamb, caught in the grips of the wolf—the enemy of us all.

But other children have been delivered from their tormentors and are now glowing with the peace of the Lord. Yes, a child can be saved and used of God!

When I was nine years of age, I accepted Christ as Savior, so I know first-hand that a child can be

THEY DESERVE A SECOND CHANCE

saved. My baby sister, Carolyn, and my brother, Wayne, less than two years older than I, were baptized in a creek near New Home Free Will Baptist Church in Tulsa, Oklahoma, on the same day. We are all living for the Lord.

Our three children were born M.K's (missionary kids) in Brazil and I saw first-hand through them that God can save and use children at a very early age.

Our five-year-old, Kemper, came to me in his pajamas early one morning and said, *"Mamae, quero Jesus no coracao.*

"You want Jesus in your heart? Oh, how wonderful!"

We went over the plan of salvation together and prayed. When he raised his head, tears were in his eyes and in mine. Our son was praying the same prayer I had used with children since I started teaching Sunday school in the seventh grade.

He ran to his father, *"Pai,* we need to call the United States!"

"Why son?"

"We need to call Grandma and Grandpa in Oklahoma and Papaw and Mamaw in West Virginia and tell them that I got saved. They'll be so happy!"

We had a seminary intern staying at our house and Kemper kept asking him, *"Francisco, esta feliz?"*

"Sim, Kemper, I am happy."

"I am too, because I asked Jesus into my heart."

After we went to bed, we could hear Kemper talking, "Francisco, are you still happy?"

"Yes, Kemper, I am."

Later, "Francisco, are you happy?"

"Sim, Kemper, but don't you think you need to sleep now?"

"Okay. *Boa noite* (goodnight)."

"Boa noite."

"I'll be happy tomorrow, too."

THEY DESERVE A SECOND CHANCE

His "tomorrows" included growing up in Brazil, attending Hillsdale Free Will Baptist College, *Seminario Batista Livre,* and the University of Central Oklahoma where he graduated with a degree in Decision Sciences. He serves his Jesus in Brazil as a Sunday school teacher, youth sponsor, and through an instrumental and vocal ministry. He also serves on the board of the Children's Home.

During one of our furloughs, our second child, Cindy, was about six-years-old and listening to a gospel record for children. It was a story about a little boy who hid a snake that grew up and killed his dog and then bit him. Cindy ran into the room where I was and said, "Mama, I need to pray and get saved."

"Okay, honey, we can do that now."

"Billy hid his sins about the snake and I need to ask forgiveness and get saved, too!"

We knelt beside the bed as she prayed her prayer of repentance. As soon as she finished she said, "Let's call Daddy in California and tell him." Her father had been gone for four weeks in missionary conferences.

"I want Daddy to help Brother Pirtle baptize me." So as soon as her father returned to Oklahoma, she was baptized. The heater had gone out of the baptistery on that cold day in October, but she was determined to be baptized anyway!

She grew up in Brazil, attended the *Seminario Batista Livre,* Hillsdale Free Will Baptist College, and then returned to Brazil to graduate from *Faculdade Sao Luis.* She married a Brazilian deacon in the church who studies law. She is now a mother. She and her husband, Jose Augusto, work faithfully in their local church, and she has taught in the Brazilian Bible College. She visits the Children's Home often and tells the children stories like "Billy

THEY DESERVE A SECOND CHANCE

and the Snake."

Our youngest daughter, Tania, told me one Sunday in Brazil that she wanted to accept Christ that night.

"Sweetheart, you don't have to wait until tonight, you know."

"Oh, I want to wait until tonight, *mamae.*"

That night she sat close to me and reminded me what she had planned to do. After a while I noticed just how quiet she was—she was asleep!

"Oh, well," I mused, "she is only seven and she must accept Christ when she is ready"

At the end of the closing hymn, she woke up and looked around. Her father was saying the benediction.

"Mamae," she tugged at my skirt, "I'm supposed to get saved tonight."

"You went to sleep, sweetheart. You can do it at home," I comforted her.

"No, I want to do it here and tonight."

She walked up to the front and knelt down at the altar her grandfather had made on his last trip to Brazil. I whispered to Jim what had happened and he called the people who were visiting to order.

"What is Tania doing?" they were asking.

Our Brazilian Christians had made decisions in their home and since it was a new work, they had never seen anyone kneel at the altar in a church before. Since Tania had been born in Brazil, we couldn't remember where she had seen it done that way! But as she arose from the altar, our tiny blond-haired daughter had tears streaming from her blue-green eyes. Many other brown eyes were swimming with tears, also.

Tania was baptized in the outside baptistery under the banana trees along with other Brazilians.

THEY DESERVE A SECOND CHANCE

She grew up in Brazil, then attended Hillsdale Free Will Baptist College where she received an A.A. degree and then went to the University of Central Oklahoma to finish her business course. She has a special gift in music—voice and guitar—and a special way to get people "moving" in our church activities in Brazil. Many times her bedroom has made room for active little girls who were curious about her fair skin, the color of barriga de peixe (fish's belly), and admired her willingness to share her home and parents with them. Can a child find forgiveness and salvation in Jesus Christ? Oh yes, and that is our main source of hope for suffering, wounded children all over the world who have not really had a chance to be children.

Satan wants to destroy our children. That has been his tactic since the first murder among young brothers.

What did Pharaoh do in the Old Testament to stop God's plan? He ordered the Hebrew children to be killed.

What did Herod do in the New Testament to stop God's plan? He ordered the slaughter of children.

What is the sacrifice used in many cultic rituals in the past and today? Little children.

What tactic is Satan using today in our beloved United States and in Brazil? Abortion!

Yes, a child can be used by Satan and filled with his evil, but God created us to be filled with His love and His Spirit.

It is okay that children arrive at our Children's Home wounded. They can be lame, spotted and not perfect. But praise God, they don't have to be, for their Good Shepherd was also the perfect Sacrificial Lamb that "takes away the sin of the world." He gave His life for His sheep and they know His voice.

THEY DESERVE A SECOND CHANCE

For this reason we will continue to search the streets for wounded lambs and place them in the arms of the Good Shepherd.

THEY DESERVE A SECOND CHANCE

CHAPTER SIX

THE FIRST RESCUE

HEADLINES:

Death Squads, perhaps moonlighting police officers, rid neighborhoods of "social undesirables" by **killing street children.**

"Pest Controls" hired by local businesses are executing street children who are seen as thieves and criminals.

Seven more street children assassinated in city square last night!

Bruises and scars from the many beatings were visible on the thin, little arms of the child as he buried his head in them. He surrendered to sobs and cried, "I'll never be able to do it. Never!" He yielded to the sobs that had been locked inside him since that awful day two years before and the many terrible days since then. That day was locked inside him, but it came out through screams during his nightmares or it was expressed in his fear to be seen in the street by day.

The policeman had found him this time beaten almost unconscious by his stepfather who accused him of being lazy and not bringing home enough money after a day of begging in the streets.

THEY DESERVE A SECOND CHANCE

The police officer confided to me before we were given the child, "You need to understand something else besides these beatings he is receiving. When he was six years of age, he was raped. Now he is so introverted that he can't approach people in the streets to beg."

"What about his mother?"

"She has two younger children by this man who inflicted the beatings and she is an alcoholic. We told her to choose between the man and her boy. She chose the man."

And now he was with us, tormented by this rejection, the first child sent to us even before the official opening of the Children's Home.

"I'll never be able to read and write," he mumbled as he lifted his head.

"Why do you say that, Jose? Sure you can," encouraged Marcos, one of the volunteers in the home.

"Nobody big in my family can read. My mama can't read. I don't know anybody big who can read." The pencil trembled in his slender fingers.

This conversation was taking place only days after we opened *La^y Nova Vida*. The sobbing, wounded child was being comforted by a young man who was an ex-street child himself. God had sent him to live with us seven years before when we lived in another city.

After being rescued from the streets, Marcos and Jose had a long way to go, but by the grace of God, they had escaped the death squads who were killing Brazil's street children. They had escaped nights of sleeping under cardboard in dark, cold alleys. Marcos could be confident that Jose could have a new life because of what God had done for him years before.

THEY DESERVE A SECOND CHANCE

MARCOS' STORY

The Rescue

The weary little mother carefully laid the tiny baby in the cloth-lined shoe box resting on a makeshift twin-size bed. Makeshift. That could describe the patched-up walls of the dark little shanty, the table leaning against the wall on its remaining three legs, and the rocks and blackened bricks forming a circle on the dirt floor. The provisional "stove" awaited a fire and a pot of water to boil the last bit of food in the house—a package of spaghetti.

The boy, Marcos Antonio, would not notice that there as nothing to put on the spaghetti except for some damp salt and stale vegetable oil from the bottom of a can found in a nearby dump. He would satisfy his first of many hunger pangs with the warm maternal liquid given to him by his young mother as long as she had strength to produce her milk. This would quiet his tears and she could place him again, sleeping peacefully, in his little shoe-box crib.

Quiet. Peace. Rare ingredients in this little scene so typical of many of the poor in Brazil. The child's father, a favorite among the neighborhood vacant-lot soccer fans, was a sometime painter, but a full-time alcoholic. He loudly and aggressively demanded peace, quiet and anything else that might come into his arguments in his regular drunken rages.

The baby outgrew his little shoe box and was placed on a makeshift bed—a folded blanket in a darkened corner. He outgrew his maternal milk feedings and discovered the taste of that spaghetti seasoned with damp salt and old vegetable oil. As he grew, he learned to carry buckets of water for his mother as she cleaned houses for others. Then he watched the kind

THEY DESERVE A SECOND CHANCE

women pay her for her labor with a warm sweater for her bright little boy, or a portion of food and a few *centavos* for the day's work. He also knew the money would probably go to buy the cheap white lightning to appease his father when he came home late at night, and to satisfy the drinking habit his mother had acquired through her hollow despair.

Marcos would later look back on certain times as almost tender moments when he would sit (at a safe distance, of course) and listen to his folks talk about old times, share funny stories and personal adventures. He absorbed their handed down, home-spun knowledge and opinions on animals, plants, personal relationships and the oppressive religious rituals that filled their lives and those of many others around them.

But these moments were very few. His days were more likely filled with hunger, disease and physical and verbal abuse. Since all the bad situations in his young, sad life seemed to come from within the crumbling walls of their little shanty, he went to the streets. His father repeatedly threatened the child and told him to go away. So he did. Away from the beatings and raging verbal abuse. Away from the empty shelves and molded food. Away from the vengeance of a disturbed parent and the demons behind the family, idols.

Later he would discover that the street—which falsely promised him recreation, income, education and the comradeship of other castaways—was really a trap for crime. Stealing or begging. Paying for protection from comrades. Drugs, prostitution, disease. Sleeping under bridges and in deserted corners. Hiding and running. A lifetime of illiteracy. And for many children it meant DEATH. Frustrated business people would hire moonlighting policemen to kill these little gangs

THEY DESERVE A SECOND CHANCE

of children who stole from them and terrorized their customers.

How does a child like this have a chance? What can turn around such wretched facts to offer any hope of change?

Well, a chocolate Easter egg, for a start.

Chocolate Easter Egg

"Marcos," a friend called to him one day, "let's go to that little *Batista Livre* church Sunday. It's right down the street and I hear they give chocolate eggs for Easter."

What luck! Not only could he get delicious chocolate for his very own, but his only T-shirt was spread out on a nearby bush drying in the hot Brazilian sun. For some reason, clean clothes were important for such an occasion. A rickety faucet exposed in an empty lot furnished water for his daily wash-ups after the night's darkness blanketed him with privacy. Pieces of used soap were easy to find in trash sacks and they supplied his bath, shampoo and laundry needs. Rubber thongs would have been nice, but he knew his friend wouldn't have any either.

"Sure, I'll go with you," he answered his waiting playmate. One of many decisions that changed his life.

Easter Sunday found the boys shyly entering the yard of the mission church. They were met with warm greetings from smiling adults. Unlike other adults who ran them away from their properties, these adults ushered them right up to the front of the church into choice seats where other squirming children were seated.

Some of those same young adults were up front with instruments—guitars, tambourines, and maracas—singing some of the happiest music Marcos had ever heard. The young people, using

THEY DESERVE A SECOND CHANCE

figures on a flannel board, told the story about a loving Father who saw His Son nailed to a cross. This caught Marcos' attention.

"A loving Father," he meditated. "We had an idol in our house with the dead Christ on the cross. Another had the 'queen mother' Mary, with her crown and robes and the dead son at her feet."

They went on, "God the Father loved the world—you boys and girls here—so much that He gave His Son to die on the cross.

Marcos reflected, "Somebody loves me? These people surely are nice to me."

A beautiful angel figure sitting on a stone in front of a cave was placed on the flannel board.

"But this Son didn't stay dead. He arose from the dead. He's alive! He is not dead on a cross. He's alive! That's why we are celebrating today. Come back tonight, and we will continue our celebration."

It was time to line up and receive the chocolate eggs as part of the day's festivities. Marcos and his friend walked out that Sunday with their prized chocolate wrapped in shiny paper.

"*Oba*, Marcos, let's remember to come back next year," his friend beamed.

"*Vou voltar hoje a noite,*" he answered his friend seriously. "You're coming back tonight? You're *loco!* There won't be any more chocolate tonight."

"I don't care. Didn't you like the music? Weren't they nice people? They invited us back tonight." He did not mention that he was curious to know more about the story he had heard. A story about a loving Father.

"Naw, I'm going to play soccer. We need you too, *amigo*. Come on."

But the two friends parted and Marcos stuck true to his decision, a decision that changed the course of his life.

SHIRLEY ALBERTA COMBS

THEY DESERVE A SECOND CHANCE

He was still a child, still scratching out a daily survival. But he had new friends and he met a real friend, Jesus, who became his Savior and Lord. Little Marcos was faithful to congregate with the folks at the small mission church. He also talked with his friends and invited church neighbors to attend the services.

With his newfound joy and the bundle of clothes his new friends had given him, the boy went back to his little shanty to tell his mother and father about his friend, Jesus. His mother listened, curious, but reluctant. His father looked at the things in his bundle and said nothing. But he didn't tell him to leave, either.

At about this time, 1985, Jim and I started helping the young people at the Ipiranga mission in Ribeirao Preto, Brazil. We met Marcos and other children attending the services. Jim had the privilege of baptizing Marcos and a friend, Sebastiao, in the little baptistery revealed by lifting the floor of the tiny stage at the front of the church.

Broken Idols-Burned Bible

One day Marcos didn't show up at Sunday school—unusual for him. Enough people made comments about problems at his home that I became concerned. Jim had obligations in another church that day, so I asked one of the young leaders, Caesar, a veterinarian, to go with me to Marcos' house after church. We prayed together in the car before we approached the house.

A small man answered our clapping outside the shack by opening the door and staring at us.

"*Senhor,* we are from the church and came by to visit with you folks and Marcos. May we come in?" My voice was calmer than I had felt a few seconds before.

THEY DESERVE A SECOND CHANCE

He looked silently back into the dark room and then at us. He motioned for us to enter. The boy was there standing by his mother who was seated at the table in the only visible chair. Blood was running down her neck from a gash in the back of her head.

As my eyes adjusted to the darkness, I saw the smoke-stained wall, the stones on the floor that served as a cook stove and the barrenness of the room.

"Senhor, we have come here as friends. We don't know you but have learned to love your son, and he has been concerned for his family. I hear things are going on here. Could we talk about them?"

He spoke for the first time, looking toward the wall, "This boy comes in here talking about strange religions. He took my gods off the shelf and broke and burned them."

Marcos held his head down, but it sounded just like him in his new-found zeal.

"I hear you burned his Bible and his clothes. Can you tell me why you did that?"

"Maldicao! A curse! That's what that Bible is. Ever since he brought that Book into this house, only evil has come to us." His voice was rising and arms swinging. I moved between him and Marcos.

"What about his clothes?" I ventured.

"He should be bringing in things for us, for me. All he thinks about is himself and that church, so I burned them and everything else, too."

Caesar had been praying silently as I spoke to them. Now he was speaking and it was my turn to claim protection and power in the name and blood of Jesus Christ. He calmly, lovingly told the beautiful story of the gospel, and it had never sounded as hopeful, as complete, as simple and as powerful as it did to me in that setting of darkness.

Caesar checked the head wound on the woman and we exchanged the polite good-byes required in

THEY DESERVE A SECOND CHANCE

that culture, for we had to leave them and Marcos with the promise to see him that night.

But I have never been able to leave that scene. It influenced personal decisions and personal commitments we would face.

THEY DESERVE A SECOND CHANCE

THEY DESERVE A SECOND CHANCE

CHAPTER SEVEN

A SECOND CHANCE

Sleeping in the Streets

Sometime later, one of our Brazilian leaders, Cecilia, came to us with a question: "Did you know Marcos is sleeping in the streets? Recently he has been sleeping in the rest room behind the church." Later Marcos told me he had slipped through a broken windowpane each night and out of the church each morning.

Bothered by that information, I went home and talked it over with Jim and we discussed it with the children. Jim thought Marcos could help mail out Bible correspondence courses—a time-consuming ministry with about 200 participating students. It required standing in long lines at the post office. In fact, Jim thought he could have him stand in a few more long lines built into the Brazilian culture. We could make him a bed down in a tiny room Jim was using as an office and put his few belongings in a file cabinet drawer. We could pay the lad a minimum salary and give him room and board. Our family agreed and we invited another person to join our family.

Marcos also agreed and showed up at our gate barefooted and carrying a bundle of clothes too small for him. We had clothes and shoes ready for him.

He was full of surprises. When Jim lined up the office work for him to do, we discovered he

THEY DESERVE A SECOND CHANCE

couldn't read or write! He had good grammar, a wide vocabulary and was a good conversationalist. We had just not thought about his not being able to read or write.

"Son, why didn't you go to school?"

"I enrolled one time but they wouldn't let me stay."

"Why not?"

"I don't have a birth certificate."

"No problem. We'll get you one. When is your birthday?" "I don't know."

"Okay. No problem again. We'll ask your mother." "She doesn't know either."

He was small for his age, maybe because he thought he was about 12 or 13 years old.

"As long as you live here you are going to school young man." And with that, my determined husband's battle with bureaucratic red tape and uncooperative people began.

He finally won the battle and proudly presented Marcos with a birth certificate. The boy had chosen a Brazilian holiday, July 9, as his birthday and his mother had chosen 12 as his age.

He enrolled in school, learned to read and write and charmed his way into the hearts of our family. He became one of our own—bringing joy, frustration, and delight. But he was one of ours.

Little did we know that one day he would be helping us in a ministry to many more street children.

We all knew that taking a child from the streets and placing him in a middle-class home of foreigners was not a common scenario. As a Brazilian saying translates, we were "new sailors on our first voyage," so we tried to discuss basic guidelines as to what we imagined could happen. We prayed to have daily wisdom to help this young man

THEY DESERVE A SECOND CHANCE

have a new chance in life. Our two main goals for our new son were schooling and a profession.

Reading and Writing and ... What?

He was a naturally bright child so he learned to read and write quickly and mastered other subjects as well, except for math. At that time, if you failed in one subject you had to repeat the whole year. We offered to get him a tutor, but he kept saying, "No, the next time I'll get better. I just need to apply myself more."

Semester after semester he struggled with math and it was an exciting day when he called me into his bedroom where he had his homework spread out on his bed.

"Look at this. I've learned to divide by three numbers!" he beamed as he placed the notebook in my hands.

It was true. In very neat writing, the page was filled with division problems, all correct. Here was our grown-up, handsome, chocolate colored, muscular son needing a mother's approval of a job well-done. One more small victory to help him over life's hurdles.

The Light of Integrity

Another hurdle was a profession. As opportunities came up, we allowed him to take on jobs that interested him. He is a "sanguine" who faces short-term goals with enthusiasm. He started out as an office boy helping us in our own time-consuming ministries. We felt he needed to work where he would be responsible to others. He studied at night so his days were free to work.

With his natural restlessness and the fact that we have moved several times since he came to live with us, he has had a variety of jobs. In the second city where we lived, he worked at a filling station, a

THEY DESERVE A SECOND CHANCE

car wash and a ceramic factory. When we moved to the third city, he worked as a gardener for a florist, in direct sales and in a jeans factory until it closed down. Recently the inflation in Brazil has been 2,000 percent a year, and the minimum salary about $80 a month. Most of his jobs were minimum wage jobs.

In each situation Marcos witnessed to people at work, and he was always commended for his Christian stand. However, his Christian integrity cost him his favorite job.

When he was about 20, Marcos was hired by a transport company contracted by a yogurt factory, part of the Nestle company in Araras. He had a strong body, was not lazy and had a winning personality. One man from our church who worked at the factory commented, "They love Marcos at the plant. He'll have a job as long as he wants it."

But Marcos observed certain procedures by drivers of the transport company that disturbed him. Then they started requiring him to unload damaged goods hidden among the boxes or to falsify delivery reports. He refused to do this and the drivers wrote up "uncooperative" reports on him.

After several of these reports crossed the desk of the main boss, Marcos was called in.

"Marcos, you have been a good employee. You are working under the authority of our drivers and you need to be cooperative."

"I am cooperative, as much as possible." He hated to cost the drivers their jobs by telling about the dishonest deliveries and reports.

"Well, it is possible. You must do what they say."

He breathed a prayer and with a heavy heart told his boss the whole sad story. He said he knew the Nestle Company would not want its customers being deceived and he could not participate in the drivers' activities.

THEY DESERVE A SECOND CHANCE

"You don't work for the Nestle Company. You work for our transport company. Just do what you are told."

"Do you mean that I have to be dishonest to work for your company?"

"You have to do what your boss tells you to do."

At that point he realized that he was not costing the drivers their jobs. He could lose his own job.

"Then I can't work for you anymore." He sadly left the office and the job that he had enjoyed so much.

Then he was faced with the job of telling us about one more failure. For us it was a great sign—that, given a chance, a child can develop into a Christian man who faces life's problems with integrity.

THEY DESERVE A SECOND CHANCE

> THEY DESERVE A SECOND CHANCE

CHAPTER EIGHT

A CALL TO BATTLE

Discerning the Spirits

Marcos participated in the music program of the church and was a favorite as counselor at many youth camps. He could sing, play soccer, give a testimony, act, pray, counsel and discern the spirits. The last seemed to be his special gift.

Once a young man came to the Free Will Baptist camp property, where we lived at the time, and asked for prayer. Jim prayed for him and then left him sleeping in one of the dorm rooms. Later, a terrified neighbor came screaming that a man was in our yard trying to cut himself with a knife. Jim jumped up, but Marcos had already disappeared. By the time Jim arrived at the scene, Marcos had the man on his knees and, in Jesus' name, had already cast out the demon that had been tormenting his victim.

Trouble on the Bus

Another time, Marcos was traveling on a public bus. From his seat near the back he could see a woman fall out into the aisle. Several went to her aid. The bus driver parked on the side of the highway in order to investigate the commotion.

"Let this lady help her. She's a nurse,.." someone offered.

THEY DESERVE A SECOND CHANCE

All the time people were trying to help the fallen victim, it seemed to Marcos that God was telling him, "Go pray with the woman. She has a demon problem."

"Who, me, Lord? I'm just a kid!"

"Go and pray with the woman. She has a demon problem."

He got up from his seat and made his way to the front.

"May I pray with the woman? I think she has a spiritual problem."

The driver retorted, "Well, I'm for trying anything. We aren't helping her and *we* need to get back on the road!"

Marcos prayed in the name and through the blood of Jesus Christ. Immediately, the woman came to herself and got back into the seat. He returned to his seat and felt himself trembling as he thought about the scene he had just witnessed. "How powerful is the name of Jesus! And God used me," he meditated as the bus took off again on its journey.

He was still beaming as he told the story to us later that night.

Fallen Classmate

One night in his evening class, a classmate fell to the floor in some kind of fit. The director of the school and others were trying to revive the woman and remove her from the area.

Marcos approached the director and asked, "May I pray with the woman? She may have a spiritual problem."

The director, an ex-priest, waved him away, "No way. This is not a spiritual problem. Go on back into your classroom."

Marcos returned to his room and sat at his desk impressed to pray for the fallen classmate. After several moments, a person arrived at the classroom

THEY DESERVE A SECOND CHANCE

door and asked the teacher to send Marcos to the director. He went, not knowing what to expect, but found the director with the unconscious classmate on the floor.

"We've tried everything we know to do. Go ahead and pray for her," he motioned Marcos toward the woman.

He knelt by the woman, but looked up at the director.

"Before I pray, I want you to know that whatever happens here will come from the power of God, and not anything I do. Do all of you witnessing this understand that God's power is about to be manifested?"

"Yes, we understand."

Marcos prayed with courage and asked in the name of Jesus and through His blood that God would do what he had seen Him do many times before, cast out the evil spirit that was tormenting and controlling the woman.

She immediately awoke from her trance and they helped her up. Marcos explained to her what had happened and that God had freed her. In order to remain free from her tormentor she needed to accept Christ and fill herself with God's Holy Spirit.

As a result of this incident, the director gave an unusual invitation to Marcos. The school was having many problems of that nature, plus incidents of drug problems, absenteeism and fighting's. He told Marcos that he could take a class period every Friday night to talk with the students. Several times he rented gospel films (the teachers and students even offered to help pay for them) and invited instrumental groups of professional people from our church. They presented music, antidrug programs and gave testimonies of God's power to transform lives.

THEY DESERVE A SECOND CHANCE

Back to the Streets

He and a friend from the church walk the streets on Saturday nights and hand out tracts to "night people." Marcos listens to their problems, prays for them and invites them to church. The two young men choose a different section each Saturday and work the streets until dawn. Then, they go straight to church and wait until Sunday school. A few of the couples and other adults, now a part of the church, were won to the Lord by Marcos during the Saturday night vigils.

The life of this young man came around full circle when our local church in Araras opened the work among street children. He understood the children and could do more with them than anyone. They loved, respected and admired him for being a brave Christian young man.

He comforted them through the nights as they screamed from nightmares or memories of reality. He helped to nourish them to health as they overcame their wounds and diseases. He helped them get dressed in the mornings, walked them to school and talked to their teachers about individual needs and situations. He helped the police find runaways and protected the children from belligerent relatives and threatening gang leaders. He helped them with their homework and prayed with them about the hurt they had in their hearts toward people who beat them, sent them away or abandoned them to survive on their own.

He encouraged them to study and learn when it seemed impossible. That's why he was helping Jose (Chapter 6) when the boy had concluded, "I'll never be able to read and write." He knew how Jose felt for he had been given a chance and had learned!

He shared with the children how it was possible to forgive parents and others who had wronged

THEY DESERVE A SECOND CHANCE

them, for he had been. Able to forgive his own parents.

And very important, he taught them that when they became responsible adult citizens, they also must give other children a chance to dream and to fulfill their dreams. He had been given a chance, and his dreams were coming true.

Now Jose and the others can dream as every child has a right to do. He did learn how to read, plant a garden and care for bunny rabbits. He learned to sleep through the night without the screaming nightmares—all in the security of a loving Christian environment called New Life Children's Home. But it wasn't always like that.

THEY DESERVE A SECOND CHANCE

This is the Free Will Baptist Church in Araras, S.P., Brazil.

Spiritual Life

Missionary Jim Combs baptizes one of the older children.

The children participate in the "booster band" at church.

THEY DESERVE A SECOND CHANCE

All school-age children from the home are enrolled in public schools.

Education

Marcos helps a child with homework. Most have not been in school before and need special training.

CHORES: The children learn to work together, and they learn the importance of fulfilling responsibility.

Activities

HEALTHY SMILES: We are fortunate to have volunteer dentists and doctors to help.

THEY DESERVE A SECOND CHANCE

BIG SOCCER FANS: The children need to spend their energy somewhere!

PARTIES: It is important to replace bad memories with happy ones. Some have never had a birthday cake before.

THEY DESERVE A SECOND CHANCE

Shelter

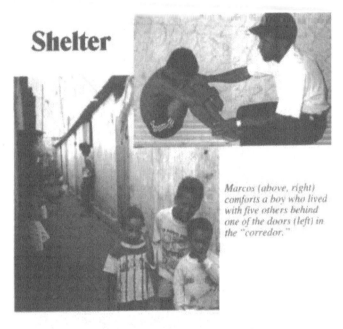

Marcos (above, right) comforts a boy who lived with five others behind one of the doors (left) in the "corredor."

Two of our children came from this location.

THEY DESERVE A SECOND CHANCE

FIRST RENTED HOUSE: It was a "a good idea."

FUTURE SITE: Pastor Eliseu inspects the land donated for the future home.

THEY DESERVE A SECOND CHANCE

Siblings

These five brothers and sisters came to the home.

Five more brothers and sisters also came to the home.

We asked for a bicycle and God sent us a Volkswagen van . . . and then two bicycles.

THEY DESERVE A SECOND CHANCE

Bright faces indicate these siblings have found hope at the home as they have been "grafted" together as a family.

Brothers

Sisters

THEY DESERVE A SECOND CHANCE

DEDICATED: Benedito and Denei are dedicated house parents.

FIRST HOUSEMOTHER: Dona Antônia was the first housemother at the home.

MARCOS, who was a street child himself, has proven to be a valuable helper with the children.

PASTOR Eliseu and his wife, Josete, have been faithful.

THEY DESERVE A SECOND CHANCE

FAMILY: *Our three Brazilian-born children Kemper, Cindy and Tânia; our son-in-law, José Augusto; and "foster son," Marcos, have all helped in the home. They have unselfishly shared their homes and parents with many little lambs.*

Workers and Volunteers

OFFICERS: *Kemper, Celina, Isabel, Yara and Luciana are officers and volunteer nurses of the Children's Home.*

THEY DESERVE A SECOND CHANCE

New Life Children's Home

By God's grace these little lambs have been rescued, but many others remain in the streets. They need prayer and the commitment of those who have the answer—Jesus Christ.

House parents and children are gathered by the New Life Children's Home.

THEY DESERVE A SECOND CHANCE

The Younger the Better

Shirley holds a child on his day of arrival, a scary experience for a two-year-old.

"Uncle Pastor" Jim usually has both knees occupied at the home.

SHIRLEY ALBERTA COMBS

Special Programs

Participation helps to build self-worth in little ones who have been rejected and abused.

THEY DESERVE A SECOND CHANCE

PART-TWO
MIRACLE STORY

THEY DESERVE A SECOND CHANCE

THEY DESERVE A SECOND CHANCE

CHAPTER NINE

THE BEGINNING

These "miracle stories" of lambs being rescued could not have been told without the people who caught a vision and acted. And God's promises and guidance were primary in making things happen at the right time and in the right places.

New Life Children's Home didn't just happen and it hasn't always been there! Many street children were suffering and losing their lives. They had nowhere to go! Unfortunately, we didn't realize the seriousness of their plight and we had no idea we could do anything to change the circumstances. But God knew!

Death Squads

After many of the Araras church members participated in a course on evangelism, they developed a growing concern for neighbors around the church building who never visited the services. Those who lived next door and across the street from the church had never entered the church door. How could we get their attention?

We decided to try to fulfill some need in their lives. Since it was a middle-class neighborhood, they didn't need soup lines like the many poor areas. They didn't need clothing or the weekly agape food baskets our church distributed.

With yearly inflation of 2,000 percent times were tough for middle class families. Public schools didn't and still don't offer typing classes, home economics,

THEY DESERVE A SECOND CHANCE

music classes or computer courses. All of these are provided through private classes. But at that time private classes were getting more difficult to afford.

An idea was forming which resulted in our placing a huge banner in the trees on the church lawn. It read:

FREE CLASSES HERE
Computer classes—Guitar classes—Oil painting—Chess-
Textile painting—Manicure course—Hair cutting course-
Crochet—Knitting
Enrollment: Tuesday evening
Classes: Monday-Tuesday-Thursday-Friday

We explained to the neighbors that we would have an hour of class, 15 minutes of devotion and then another hour of class. Since most neighbors were Spiritists or Catholics, we explained that a "devotion" meant a story from the Bible, a song and a prayer. They said they understood.

On the night of enrollment we did not know what to expect. Neighbors started filing in. Adults, adolescents and children. Forty neighbors were gathered in the church for free classes. More people came for devotional time than for the classes!

It was an exciting time for our church. Only a few of those who took courses actually integrated full-time into our church family, but the neighbors around the church have never been friendlier.

One neighbor remarked, "I've lived here for years and this is the first time this church has ever done anything." However, the man had not seen the people who had accepted Christ, the lives that had been changed. Nor did he know of the broken homes which had been mended and reunited through the healing of forgiveness. But what he had seen was a group of caring people reaching out to him and his neighbors and fulfilling needs.

Visit to City Hall

The church was excited over the multi-ministry efforts in the neighborhood and felt they could do more for the community.

Since the church had several teachers, nurses and other professional people, someone suggested we consider opening a free Christian day care center in a poor neighborhood. We decided to check with people at city hall about the most strategic location for such a center. A surprise was waiting at city hall.

Margarida wove her little Volkswagen Beetle in and out of the busy traffic of cars, bicycles, motorcycles, horses and wagons, mothers pushing baby buggies and especially jay-walking pedestrians. "What do you think she will tell us?" Margarida asked.

"I just don't know, but from the nervousness I'm feeling, you would think she had called us instead of our calling her."

Luckily, we found a parking place by the time *Senhor Jose* was opening the doors and putting out the Brazilian flag in front of the renovated historic building. We made our way over the cobblestone streets, swirl-designed stone sidewalks and then up the highly polished old wooden steps to the receptionist's desk. We were in for a life-changing surprise.

"Bom dia, Dona Shirley. Dona Olga is expecting you." The receptionist showed us into the beautiful high-ceilinged chambers and soon we were seated in front of *Dona Olga.*

Dona Olga, the director of the Department of Human Services, had scheduled a meeting with Margarida, a school teacher, and me that afternoon

THEY DESERVE A SECOND CHANCE

to hear the church's idea about opening a free Christian day care center. We were sent there by the church to get the city's suggestion on its location. She listened politely and then said, "Araras is a model city for day care centers. We have new, modern centers that aren't even full yet. Would you consider doing something else for the community?"

"We had mentioned the possibility of working with the elderly or maybe with street children in the future ......

"That's it," she interrupted, "we have a great need for someone to work with street children. We have children sniffing glue. We have children giving birth to children and giving drugs to their babies. These children are in the streets begging, forming gangs and stealing, especially from downtown shops. They are abused and beaten at home so they flee to the streets for their entertainment, education and what they think is safety."

My heart seemed to be thudding in my chest and throbbing in my neck at the same time. Margarida glanced over at me.

"Father," I breathed as she continued on, "what is she saying here? Is it possible that this is a direction we should consider? This is no small responsibility and we are a small group."

We had heard, of course, on national news that children's gangs were so numerous and strong in some large cities that business people were hiring moonlighting policemen to shoot these street children. Headlines in the morning newspapers often read like these: "Seven more children found shot in the city square last night," and "Street children considered social undesirables are being executed."

In the state of Rio de Janeiro alone, 306 children were killed in 1991, 424 in 1992, in 1993 estimates

THEY DESERVE A SECOND CHANCE

range from 560 to 855, and during the first three months of 1994 some 234 children were believed to have been killed by extermination squads.

Our church had been seeing the same problem on a smaller scale locally but was at a loss to know what to do.

Weekly agape food baskets were given to the poor from our church but they only represented immediate relief with no social reform and no lasting help.

Dona Olga was continuing, "Would your church consider such a project?"

My reply reflected my thoughts: "We are a small group to take on such a task."

"Yes, I know your group. My son now attends your church since you started the classes for the neighborhood."

"Yes, we know Marcio. He is a special friend of our family now," I offered.

"Our family has been changed since our son started attending your church," she confided. "He is calmer and more satisfied and we always know where he is—at church! But back to the street children."

She explained that they had offered the Catholic groups and Spiritist groups help with such a project if they would accept it. These two groups in our city are very strong and involved in charity organizations. At that time, they did not think they had personnel or a program to deal with such children and their particular needs.

The city was willing to rent a house, furnish most of the food and a worker until 4 p.m. on five weekdays. She asked if we could handle the project under these conditions.

"I think we can find the necessary personnel. Although we have not had experience in this particular area, I know of one program that can

THEY DESERVE A SECOND CHANCE

work. If we accept the city's help, you cannot tie our hands on this aspect. The program would be to introduce each child to a personal relationship with Jesus Christ and a loving God. If they are going to say 'no' to drugs and crime they must have an inner strength. We would provide care for their physical, intellectual and emotional needs, but true success will come with a spiritual change in their lives."

"Oh, I believe religion is important to everyone," she offered in agreement.

"Yes, but this is more than religion," I explained to her. "This is a personal relationship with Christ. These children need a second chance. A new life. A transformation."

She sighed and looked at us with the expression of a person who takes seriously the social needs of her community. "I know we have sent psychiatrists, medical people and educators to them and they have not been able to reach these children."

"Give us three months to pray about this," I responded. "During this time we can prepare a program and draw together a support group. We can see if it's possible to supplement these offers you have made. After this time, and with God's wisdom, we will try to come up with an answer."

Margarida and I left together in her little Volkswagen car, feeling so different from an hour earlier. What a change that challenge was to make in our church, community and in my own life.

THEY DESERVE A SECOND CHANCE

CHAPTER TEN

LIKE WALKING ON THE WATER

"Seven more died today! If we don't start a children's home, who will?"

"In my *opiniao,* the rest will be just like walking on water! There is no way we can predict the future and cover all the bases with guarantees."

Church members volunteered to form a committee. The history-making group consisted of the following people: Carlos, a factory owner and industrialist; Laercio, a businessman and industrialist; William, an industrial chemist; Jose, a policeman; Luis, an accountant; Regina, a retired teacher and principal; Efigenia, a retired teacher and officer in a senior citizen organization; Margarida, a teacher; Sirley, a teacher; Carmen, a philanthropist and doctor /politician's wife; and Jim and Shirley Combs, missionaries.

For three months we studied the feasibility of starting a home for street children. Visits were made to regular orphanages in the cities of Pirassununga, Limeira and Ribeirao Preto. Phone calls were made to Baptist homes for street children in the state of Parana and they graciously sent copies of their constitution and papers on internal affairs. They strongly encouraged us to pursue this ministry.

The committee worked on what they called a confirmation list which included the following questions:

THEY DESERVE A SECOND CHANCE

Is this ministry really needed? All on the committee were convinced there was an urgent need in our city for a home for street children. We agreed someone needed to meet that need. Our purpose was to determine if our church should attempt such a ministry.

How can we choose the children to minister to, and what can we do for them? We decided to accept children from birth to 12 years of age, sent to us by the juvenile judge. They would be housed seven days a week, 24 hours a day in a Christian family setting. All the children of school age would attend public schools with special tutoring done in the home. Psychological and physical care would be provided by local volunteer professionals.

Community awareness and pride would be enhanced through field trips and attendance at public parades and programs (without begging and stealing). We would accept children up to 12 years of age, but we would keep them as long as necessary to give them an education and training in some profession.

Moral and religious training would be given on a daily basis in the home and through church attendance, camps and retreats.

How can we find enough volunteers to carry out a program? It was incredible! Dentists, doctors, nurses and therapists encouraged us with their offers of help. The hospitals and labs offered services at no charge. Retired school teachers and student teachers offered help tutoring children.

Vegetable vendors and merchants offered to help. Women from the church offered a day a week or a few hours a week to help in the kitchen and with the laundry.

What about full-time workers? Volunteers were great but before we could go much further we needed full-time Christian workers (a couple or

THEY DESERVE A SECOND CHANCE

widow) and a way to pay them a salary.

One day at a wedding, Antonia, a Christian widow, said, *"Dona Shirley,* I hear our church is thinking about opening up a home for children. I was an orphan passed from house to house, and I always told the Lord that if He would allow me to work in a Christian orphanage I would dedicate myself to that ministry."

Praise the Lord! That was one more item marked off the confirmation list. Then she added, "By the way, I receive a pension from my deceased husband, so you don't need to pay me."

Great! Another item marked off the list and we seemed to be closer to a decision.

Where could we put all the children and workers? Since the city had offered to rent a house for us, we felt that was practically confirmed. BUT NOT SO. As we inquired at real estate firms, they declared, "No children."

While we were looking for a place, other facts surfaced.

As people found out about the church's interest in this community need, news got around to city officials. Police cars started stopping at our front gate ... with children. *"Senhores,* we aren't quite prepared to receive children yet. We haven't been able to find a house to rent yet." Jim and I had a two-bedroom home with four people, and felt it was already full.

But one by one, we heard the pitiful stories of the children: beaten and abused, begging in the streets, sleeping in the alleys, afraid to go home. We talked it over with our own children and they agreed. So we made room for each child one by one.

Since our home was getting a little overcrowded, we decided to get more serious about

THEY DESERVE A SECOND CHANCE

renting another place for the children. God seemed to be giving us so many green lights that we had to trust Him to confirm this last item on the list.

We decided surely someone in this entire city with a house for rent will think this is a *boa ideia*, a good idea.

Our committee felt that when we found a house, the many items on the list would be confirmed matching all the other green lights God seemed to be turning on. As one member of the committee put it, "The rest will be like walking on the water. We cannot predict the future and cover all the bases with guarantees."

The children were still suffering in the sea of life. We had been offered a chance to make a difference and Christ seemed to be waiting on the water with outstretched arms saying, "Come."

Now, where was that house?

THEY DESERVE A SECOND CHANCE

CHAPTER ELEVEN
WHEN HAVE WE SEEN YOU WITHOUT SHELTER?

In my purse, I carry a case for glasses. It does not contain my glasses which represent my need for corrective vision—physical sight. Inside the case is a roll of paper about 45 inches long which contains a list of miracles, answers to prayers concerning the needs of the Children's Home. It is to remind me that we are to walk by faith and not by sight.

At the first of that list are the answered prayers about the houses *(casas)* we needed in order to shelter the street children from our city of Araras. I read the following quotation in a Sunday school book, "Miracles are not the foundation for the household of faith, but they are the path that leads to it." You decide if they look like miracles to you!

First *Casa*

When receiving children from the streets, one of the first needs is shelter. The city's Department of Human Services offered to rent the first house we needed to begin receiving children. Since the police had already begun to send children to our home, we earnestly began visiting the many real estate offices in our city.

THEY DESERVE A SECOND CHANCE

Our minimum requirements included three bedrooms, two baths (one for the boys and another for the girls), a kitchen and some kind of yard. We knew we would have a limited selection. But when we heard so many house owners say "No children," we knew the selection was even more limited than we thought.

Some realtors raised their rent prices when we inquired about a house. We understood why they would think it was not in the best interest of their clients to rent to a house full of children, and street children certainly didn't have a good reputation in town! One real estate firm would see us entering their door and say, *"Se for Lar Nova Vida, nao tem nada"* ("If it's for New Life Children's Home, we don't have anything").

We added this specific request to our prayer list: someone who would think the ministry was *uma boa ideia* (a good idea) and one who would rent a house to us.

We watched and prayed.

Uma Boa Ideia

A friend, Carmen Salome, telephoned and asked us to meet her at a certain address near the church where a family was loading furniture onto their pickup truck.

"Maybe they haven't rented the house yet. Let's catch them before they leave."

A few minutes later I met her there and asked to talk to the man loading the pickup.

"Senhor," I started, "we are looking for a house to rent. Our church is opening a home for street children and we haven't found a house yet. Is this one rented? Who is the owner?"

"Sou eu (I am). You mean you want to rent my house to put a bunch of street kids in?"

"Um, yes sir, we do."

THEY DESERVE A SECOND CHANCE

"Well. . . ," he pondered a few seconds, "I think that is *uma boa ideia.* Our community needs a place for these children." Wow, just what we had put on the prayer list!

"To help you out," he continued, "I'll lower the price I was asking for the house. Let me call my wife; she's in the house."

While he explained the situation to his wife, Carmen and I waited hopefully. His wife looked from him to us, "Could you possibly use a long table and a few chairs. It's too big to fit in the farm house where we are moving."

"Senhora, we don't have even a spoon or a pillow. We would be happy to use your table!"

"Then how about a *cama* and *armarios,* also?"

How encouraging to hear this woman offer a bed and wardrobe since the house had no closets or cabinets and we had no furniture. How wonderfully God was answering this need!

The owner could only give us a contract for six months which we agreed to. Soon we collected enough donations to move in.

Choppy Waters

The water seemed smooth and firm as we began our walk of faith on the unknown sea toward Christ. After a few days, however, the waves began to churn.

Since bureaucratic red tape was delaying the completion of registration for the Children's Home, the Department of Human Services could not come through with the rent money and food they had promised. However, 50 adults took responsibility for the first months of rent and a couple from a supermarket sent boxes of items to get us started.

The widowed Christian who was to be housemother became ill, so the volunteers and I had to be on full-time duty the first weeks after opening. It was a great day when she arrived. By that time other children had arrived. We took care of nine children in that house.

Second *Casa*
More Choppy Waters

In six months we were visiting the real estate offices again to look for another house to rent. And they still said, "NO" to *Lar Nova Vida* children. As the date ending the contract drew near, the water seemed to churn even more beneath our feet. Some commented, "You should not have accepted the responsibility of all those lives. You have nine children now and the judge will be sending you more and more. Every time you move, you are going to need a bigger house!"

We kept our eyes on Jesus, kept on taking care of the children and kept praying for another rental house.

One day I was in the living room, which we had divided into an office/bedroom. A young lady walked in: "I hear you are looking for a house. My parents are selling their home and they have already moved to the city of Santos. If my father agrees, would you be interested in renting? It is only a few blocks from here and even closer to the church."

As she took me to the house and we looked around, I could hardly believe what God was doing. The house was larger. It had built-in cabinets and closets. It was summer, a few days before Christmas, and the house had a swimming pool!

The lady's father agreed to rent the house to us and lowered the rent to meet our budget guidelines. Unfortunately, he could only give us a

THEY DESERVE A SECOND CHANCE

year's contract because they needed to sell the house.

During that year the Lord sent us 10 more children to add to the nine we already had, plus temporary runaways we would keep from time to time.

Third *Casa*

Before the year's contract was up on the second rented house, we began to look for a third one. The real estate companies still were of no help. We found an old, closed up, condemned house on the main square. But the owner said it was up for sale and he was not interested in renting it.

The old house was so roomy that we offered to take it in spite of the termites, floors in ruins, stopped up plumbing, no windowpanes and 18 leaks in the roof! The city said they wouldn't rent it for us even if the owner did agree to it. He didn't agree so we waited, prayed and continued to look for something else.

One day a real estate company called and said the owner of the old house offered to rent to us for a year, but would only do a minimum amount of repairs to the house.

We proposed to the city to get volunteers for whatever was needed to get the house in a sanitary, living condition. Everyone agreed! We signed the one-year contract. The smooth, victory waters soon turned into a weekend storm.

Boisterous Winds

While the owner had his crew bricking-up some missing walls and repairing electrical wiring, we had our volunteer crew scraping floors, unstopping drains and painting. It was an exciting mess!

In the middle of the mess, we received

bewildering news. The family who had bought the rented house we were in *(casa* number two) called on Thursday and gave us until the weekend to get out. We told them we had a volunteer moving crew and a supermarket's truck to move us on any Monday we were ready. But we weren't ready. We asked them to give us at least until Monday. They would not agree. It surely was tempting to look around at the stormy waters.

However, the Lord helped us keep our feet firm on the water.

As people heard of our situation, families, strangers and friends bonded together and helped us pack while the children were in school that Friday. Little by little we got moved by the weekend!

The house still had no windowpanes, rain came in through the empty windows and old leaks (only two of the 18 leaks were fixable), but 20 people were able to weather the storm and sleep in what would be home for the next 14 months.

Three new children were sent to us by God during that time and the old house on the city square was the biggest shelter we had occupied yet.

Fourth *Casa*

The third house rented for the Children's Home was sold to a bank and was to be demolished. When the prospective buyer heard homeless children were living in the house, he was about to back out of the deal. He claimed it would be impossible to find another house and another landlord willing to rent to us.

The owner, who had become our friend after a reluctant beginning, related to the buyer that the home was willing to sign a paper saying we would do our best to be out 90 days after the deal was finalized. Based on the stories he heard of how God had helped us find other houses, the owner felt we would be able to keep our word.

For weeks we searched for a house and followed up on leads. Only a few days were left of our 90-day grace period. The church had started a 24-hour prayer chain for a house to rent. The owner of the big house and his real estate company said they would recommend us to anyone since we had been excellent renters. Still nothing.

Time was running out.

One Sunday, an out-of-town sister and brother and his family visited our church and heard the prayer request about a house for the Children's Home. Without saying anything, they went to their parents' home and talked them into renting to us. They owned a house which was up for sale. The proceeds were to be divided for their inheritance. Both of these young adults were renting houses in their cities, waiting on the sale of this house.

They took us to see it. It was much smaller than the other house. It was a normal, modern three-bedroom house with a patch of yard, but it looked good to us!

We signed a year's contract, put beds in the living room, placed cribs in the tiny kitchen and moved the kitchen to a work building in the backyard. In a few days, 28 people were moved into the house.

Donated Land for Kids and Fish

The juvenile judge was sending children to the Children's Home, so he was a great promoter of what we were trying to do in Jesus' name. He personally asked the mayor to donate property so the home could erect permanent buildings for the children. The initial program was designed to always keep the children living in small groups—house parents and not more than 10 children. One house was needed for children from birth to 12 years of age.

THEY DESERVE A SECOND CHANCE

As these children grew, we would care for them as long as necessary in order to give them an education and help them learn a profession. That necessitated a second house for the older boys and a third house for the older girls.

Months passed after the judge had made his request. The Brazilian pastor of the Araras church, Pastor Eliseu, informed the church folks that his brother, Osmar, along with other engineers would create a program of raising fish if the Children's Home were given land with water on it. The city heard about the program and donated land—over three and one-half acres with 500 feet of creek on one boundary.

This property will provide the much needed space to build the three houses projected as well as plenty of room for fish!

God truly is our refuge and our shelter. What better place to be.

* (The children's home buildings were not built on this property but on another location donated by a Brazilian Christian business man. The mayor convinced the city to give us funds to start the foundations of the homes.)

THEY DESERVE A SECOND CHANCE

CHAPTER TWELVE
MIRACLES THAT LEAD TO FAITH

"Miracles are not the foundation for the household of faith, but they are the path that leads to the door."

When children learn about God, they get down to the basics.

Is He alive? Does He know me? Does He answer my prayer?

This was important to remember when teaching faith to street children. It's difficult for them to trust anyone. The children were suspicious of movements toward them. They were used to fending for themselves ... in the streets.

They had two means of survival: begging and stealing. Of course, when we took them into the Children's Home, we did not permit them to use these means. It was frustrating to them. Even though they had their basic needs met as never before in their young lives, if they wanted quick money or a certain object, they couldn't beg for it or steal it anymore.

First, they had to consult someone about it. They were usually told the home didn't have funds for such things. Or, they could be told that God can supply their needs and they should pray about it. Either way, it was frustrating.

It didn't take them long, however, to observe

THEY DESERVE A SECOND CHANCE

that putting their request on a prayer list was a pretty super deal!

Electric Juicer

One special afternoon we were in the kitchen squeezing crates of oranges donated by a citrus company. Children and volunteers were singing, squeezing and filling up pitchers and tummies with the delicious juice.

One small boy, Eduardo, piped up, *"Tia* (aunt), we need one of these things with a motor on it."

"You mean an electric juicer?" I smiled.

"Sim, senhora, and I know they have them because I've seen them in the store windows."

"Oh sweetheart, that would be nice, but we don't have funds right now. Someone donated these hand squeezers but since God is your Father now, you can ask Him for one. If He thinks you need one, He can send it."

"Nao, nao. If God told someone to donate a simple little juicer, I guess they would obey. But nobody would obey if God told them to give us an electric one."

Wow! That did sound familiar and it may happen many times. I was tempted to wonder if I were putting God on the spot. Was I going to be embarrassed, or hinder someone's faith?

No, I had already learned that God was faithful and would supply our needs. It was very important to teach this to our little ones and to our volunteers. So, once again I reminded him, and all the other little ears listening, that God was their Father and He could supply their needs—without begging and stealing.

The very next day, a young woman clapped at the gate. Luciana, a nurse, shyly said, "For some reason I felt impressed to stop by and offer you this." She held out a box. "I actually have two *espremidores*

THEY DESERVE A SECOND CHANCE

eletricos and hope you can use it."

You can guess what it was. An electric juicer! We called Eduardo out and presented him to the lady. She was really touched to hear the story and realize that God had used her.

Eduardo's faith soared. And the faith of all the children and volunteers was increased as they witnessed the amazing outcome of the conversation in the kitchen the day before. All of us involved were reminded of how sweet it is to "walk by faith."

Bicycle, or Not?

Soon after the opening of the Children's Home, a bicycle was put on the prayer list. But instead of a bike, God sent a nine passenger Volkswagen van! At that time we had nine children. The number of children has increased and now that same van arrives at the Araras church with 25 or more people aboard. The tires seem to squat as they roll down the road.

About a year later, the Children's Home conducted a board meeting after Sunday school to discuss a particular need. When they last asked for a bicycle, God sent a van. But with the children getting older, some were working in the daytime and studying at night. They really needed a bicycle. It was agreed to put a bicycle back on the prayer list. The very next day, Monday, a call came to the home.

"My husband is the director of the Nestle Company here and we are being transferred to Sao Paulo. We'll be moving to an apartment and all of our things won't fit. Do you accept donations?"

"Certainly, *Dona Ursula.* Do you have our address?"

"Yes, but could someone come by to pick it up?"

"We have a van. What do you have to donate?"

"A bicycle."

I shared with her how we had just put it on a prayer list the day before and God was using her to answer our request. "In that case, could you use two bikes?"

We went immediately to her house and picked up two pink bicycles and many other useful things for the home.

Haircuts on Mondays

Some needs that would come up in staff meetings may not have seemed too important to some, but we learned that things which truly concerned us in caring for the children also concerned the Lord. One concern was haircuts.

A barber, *Senhor Sergio,* offered to give two free haircuts a day to our boys, but never on Mondays. On that day he and most barbers closed their shops. Since some of our boys' schedules only gave them time off on Monday afternoons, they ended up with either non-professional volunteer cuts or none at all. That concern was placed on the prayer lists: "Haircuts on Mondays."

Soon a reporter, Adelina, from one of the local newspapers came to the Children's Home to interview me about its ministry. She said she was touched to hear the stories of the children and their backgrounds. She was impressed to see the healthy, mannerly children and the clean, attractive way we kept up the Children's Home (she caught us on a good day).

After the interview, she commented, "By the way, I would like to be a volunteer here at your home. Besides being a reporter, I am also a beautician and can cut boys' and girls' hair. There is only one thing—I can only work on *segunda-feiras* (Mondays)!"

We began a friendship that day and she, her

THEY DESERVE A SECOND CHANCE

husband and two daughters began attending the Araras church.

Does God Have a Watch?

One morning the police department called: "We are sending two children to you. They were found in an abandoned shack and the neighbors say the mother skipped town."

"I understand and we'll prepare for them. Are they boys or girls and what are their ages?" I picked up a pen to jot down their estimated sizes so we could have clothes ready for them.

"They are two brothers. The youngest, Alex, is seven and his brother, Reginaldo, is ... uh ... 14. We know you receive up to 12 years of age but the brother has been doing odd jobs in order to feed them both. It's a pitiful story and we really don't know what to do," the policeman informed me.

"We do make exceptions to the 12 years of age ruling when there is a younger sibling involved," I told him. "This has been cleared through Dra. Marcia, hasn't it?" She was the lawyer appointed by the court to help us with the internments.

"Oh yes, she is the one who told us to call you. We'll take the boys there shortly."

They later arrived but Alex was not with them. He ran loose in the streets, they said, and nobody knew when he would show up. The police didn't have much hope of finding him after dark and the sun was almost setting.

I looked around at all the children listening to the conversation. "Let's go to the living room." They followed me and knelt down with me around an old scarred donated coffee table. Silence. They sensed something important was coming.

"There is a little boy out there somewhere. He is seven. The policemen are going out one more time

THEY DESERVE A SECOND CHANCE

to look for him and they want to find him before dark. Let's pray that will happen."

A six-year-old child asked, "Aunt Shirley, does God have a watch?"

Another interrupted, "Save your questions. It's getting dark."

The policeman respectfully left the room as all of us held hands, knelt and prayed for a little lost lamb. After prayer, the children went out on the veranda to wait.

Soon there were squeals and shouts as the police car parked in front of the house. As the sun was setting, a dirty little boy was welcomed into the fold.

THEY DESERVE A SECOND CHANCE

CHAPTER THIRTEEN
WHEN HAVE WE SEEN YOU HUNGRY?

One of the necessities of life is food. When a child is left to fend for himself in the streets, his physical needs suffer. It shows up in his frail frame, hollow eyes, rotten teeth, sparse hair and infested skin.

As educated people, we maintained healthy bodies with proper nourishment. But the Children's Home was faced with the responsibility of feeding these little ones in order to restore their health and sometimes guaranteeing a chance of survival.

We knew feeding the children would be one of the ministry's biggest responsibilities, and one of its largest expenses. The ancient story of multiplying the few loaves and fishes reminded us of the Lord's interest in meeting the physical needs of His human creation. His modern-day miracles for us proved He is still interested.

Five Kilos of Rice

One of my favorite stories involves rice. Eva, a cook sent by the city, informed me she had prepared the last bit of rice for the noon meal and none was left for the evening meal. We cook a five kilo sack of rice every day for the noon and evening meals. That is 11 pounds of rice. We try to have beans and rice every day whether or not we have much of anything else.

Since the meager funds we had on hand were for school supplies and uniforms, I told her, "Let's trust God to supply this need for the evening meal."

She dried her hands on her apron and declared, "Well, I go off duty at 4 p.m. and I can't work any miracles to make the rice stretch for dinner too."

Before Eva left for the day, a truck drove up from a plantation nearby. They had heard about the home and had brought a donation from their plantation. My mind raced, "Oh, could it be that God is sending the rice? What a witness that would be to Eva, who is not of our faith."

They unloaded two waist-high bags and revealed the contents—used clothing. After they left, I recorded the items in our "Thank-you Book." We were thankful for the much needed sandals and clothing.

My mind started meditating on the rice we needed for dinner. God had given the money for the school supplies. Should we use some of that money and trust Him to send more?

As I pulled the last item of clothing from the second bag, you can guess what I saw. A five kilo sack of rice.

I called, "Eva, come here and see what God has sent!"

She came in wiping her hands on her apron and when she saw the sack of rice she hugged me and exclaimed, "Well, I said that I couldn't work miracles in the kitchen, but it looks like God can!"

Other Foods

That was not the first provision God had sent nor was it the last. From the beginning, the city had promised to supply the bulk of the dry ingredients needed for the Children's Home such as powdered milk, sugar, flour, macaroni, rice, beans, etc. That would make us responsible for such items as vegetables, fruits and meats. But since the legal red tape had delayed the registration of the Children's Home, the city could not fulfill its promise for food

THEY DESERVE A SECOND CHANCE

during the early days after its opening.

The Lord smoothed the waters! Supermarket owners, Romeu and Daniela, sent us boxes of supplies to get us started. Folks sent food and produce from their gardens. Butchers sent us choice soup bones to spice up the stews.

Rainy Day Gave *Leite*

One day during a tropical rainstorm, a horse and buggy stopped in front of the Children's Home and we let the driver inside our gate onto the covered veranda.

"*Senhora,* I'm not going to make my delivery across town in this storm. I'm going to try to go back home so could you possibly use my cargo? I'll come back tomorrow and pick up the cans?"

"Well, what is your cargo?"

He apologetically said, *"Leite.* It will have to be boiled first." The kids peeping through the door yelled, "Yes, keep it, keep it!" They preferred fresh milk to the donated powdered milk we served.

"Yes, we'll keep it. You see, *senhor,* God has sent you to the door of a Children's Home and we certainly thank you and Him."

Mechanical Problems Gave *Carne*

One hot summer day a truck broke down in front of the Children's Home. It was on its way to Campinas, an hour away. The truck was not refrigerated so they asked if they could unload their cargo at the home.

"Certainly you may. How long do you need to leave it here?"

"Well, we would like to give it to you."

It was about 16 pounds of *carne* (meat)!

Muscle Men Have Soft Hearts

Some young men from a body builder's club

showed up at the door with boxes of food. They had sponsored a tournament and the entrance fee to the event was a kilo of non-perishable food for New Life Children's Home. We had not heard of the event and were surprised to have been chosen to receive the food. This really impressed our little children at the home!

Salt Turns into Suds

Students at a dental college in Araras had a door-to-door campaign against hunger. They delivered a small pickup truck load of goods to the Children's Home. Not only did it have food items, but it included much needed toothpaste and soap powder. We used a whole box of soap powder every day. Two hundred pounds of salt also made up part of their donations that day. When we saw *we* wouldn't be able to use it all before it collected moisture, we had a *sal da terra* (salt of the earth) campaign at church and distributed sacks of salt to the members. They brought toothpaste and soap powder to exchange for the salt. We saw salt turned into suds!

Wherefore Art Thou, Romeu?

One weekend several children were ill, as well as the governess and volunteers. Since other volunteers were Sunday school teachers, I had the home to myself. That Saturday night I finally put the last of 23 or so children to bed and I was exhausted and too numb to plan very far ahead. But I did know I would have to prepare lunch for everyone the next day, Sunday.

Plenty of food was in the pantry, but picturing myself cleaning the amount of rice and beans needed to feed my bunch and getting children ready for Sunday school at the same time made me even more exhausted.

THEY DESERVE A SECOND CHANCE

About that time I heard someone clap at the gate. It was Romeu, a businessman who had once visited our church. He explained that the Rotary Club had just finished a big meeting and wanted to give us a donation. He brought in huge pans of cooked spaghetti swimming in meat sauce, potato salad, soft drinks and the largest left-over piece of cake I had ever seen.

I couldn't even find words to thank Romeu whom God had used to take care of my particular need at that late hour. How sweet to walk with the Lord, for through sunshine or storm, He is our Jehovah Provider.

THEY DESERVE A SECOND CHANCE

THEY DESERVE A SECOND CHANCE

CHAPTER FOURTEEN

WHEN HAVE WE SEEN YOU NAKED?

"Lord, when did we see you naked?" A typical "uniform" for a street child is a thin, faded T-shirt, shorts and bare feet. When children arrive at the Children's Home, usually brought there by the police, they are met with smiles and embraces to put their suspicions at ease. We try to keep on hand a toothbrush and comb for each new child. Each child takes a hot bath (with medicated shampoo for lice) and is then given comfortable, adequate clothing and rubber thongs.

After a nourishing meal they can sleep between clean sheets on a bed by themselves, perhaps for the first time in their lives. Some come so exhausted they sleep soundly. But many have nightmares and have to be held and comforted through their screams and uncontrollable sobs.

We try to keep plenty of clothes on hand in order to dress them in clothing as nice as that of other children in the church or in school in hopes that they will not be marked as street children again.

School means uniforms, for state or private schools. Our children attend state schools and the color of their uniforms varies depending on the age of the child. Some use red and white while others choose blue and white uniforms. Each school has emblems printed on the shirts.

Many times donations will arrive with the very size and color of the uniform needed for a

THEY DESERVE A SECOND CHANCE

new child!

Mountain of Jeans

At one time, however, comment was made in a staff meeting that the jean skirts and trousers used at some of the schools where our older children attended never appeared in the donations. They are expensive to purchase so we decided to put them on the prayer list.

A few days later, a business man reported he was closing down his factory. He didn't make children's clothing but had a truckload of jeans remnants. One of our volunteers, Celina, was a seamstress with a serging machine (to overcast raw edges of material to prevent raveling) and was excited at this generous donation.

She made the needed jean skirts and pants. She also made book bags and backpacks, jean pencil holders with little zippers and drawstring bags for camps!

Out of the riches of His glory, He supplied.

Blessed Are the Feet of Them

Being below the equator, the seasons in Brazil are just the opposite of the seasons in the United States. The school year begins in March and ends in December, putting the summer vacation in January and February. By the end of summer, we start checking on the shoes-for-school situation around the Children's Home.

It used to be a battle to get the children to wear shoes, but now they appreciate being able to wear shoes to school like the other students. Each one stepped on a piece of cardboard and we drew around the foot and labeled the drawing with the child's name. They were to pray that their size would be donated in time for school to begin.

"That will take forever," the new children

THEY DESERVE A SECOND CHANCE

would complain. "You had better put your footprint on the prayer list and just wait," older children would advise them.

Once, a huge box arrived at the home. It was from *Sonia's Calcados*—a shoe store in town. It was full of canvas slip-on shoes and they offered a discount if we needed to buy sizes that were not in the box!

Then, at the beginning of summer in December, the children asked for new thongs. We had patched and wired their old ones and they were really in sad shape, but funds were shorter than usual at that time. Even before we made our cardboard drawings, a supermarket surprised us with a sackful of rubber thongs and we were able to buy the sizes that were lacking.

Angels Unaware

When the Children's Home was on the city square, a group clapped at the front gate to inquire about an address. They were from out of town so we offered the use of our telephone to help them find the people they were looking for. In talking with them, we found out that they were Christians looking for a certain family. They discovered the family had already moved from Araras.

Since we were sure they had counted on the hospitality of the Araras family for their noon meal, we offered to serve them lunch (no fast-food restaurants are in our town). Five adults and four children were in their group and we had 23 from the home. Still, we had food left over!

They thanked us and we sent them on their way with God's blessings.

Sometime later, the same group returned to

THEY DESERVE A SECOND CHANCE

Araras with fine leather boots for our boys as well as food and clothing. One of the men we had entertained on their last visit owned a factory that made quilted flannel jackets for men. He brought in arm loads of remnants that made simple blankets for the small boys' beds—and they all matched! We had entertained "angels unaware" out of our simple supplies and they had returned with God's blessings.

> THEY DESERVE A SECOND CHANCE

CHAPTER FIFTEEN

MONEY DOESN'T GROW ON ... WHAT?

As exciting as they are to receive, you cannot pay bills with sacks of rice and used sandals. Besides the cost of shelter, food and clothing, we have monthly expenses such as pharmacy bills, school supplies, light bills, phone bills and phone rental.

The church has an active women's group and they sponsor monthly projects to try to meet the bills. They have had bake sales, pizza parties and craft bazaars besides sacrificially giving of their own means and time to care for the children.

A phone in Brazil was costing from $2,000 to $5,000, depending on the current inflation rate, and the waiting list was long. Some have waited more than a year to get a purchased phone installed.

We opted to rent a phone. Due to inflation, rates were adjusted three months at a time. When the yearly inflation rate of the Brazilian economy was about 2,000 percent, that was like putting $2,000 worth of Brazilian currency under your mattress in January, taking it out in December and finding it to be worth one dollar! The first month, the phone rent in Brazilian currency would cost about US$40, and by the third month it would drop to the equivalent of about US$20.

One Thursday afternoon, our treasurer, Celina, called me and revealed, *"Dona Shirley,* the telephone rent is due tomorrow and we don't have

THEY DESERVE A SECOND CHANCE

the money in our funds. We have had a lot of sickness and our funds went for medicine."

"Do we have part of the amount?" I asked.

"No. What are we going to do?"

"How much is it?"

The amount she stated would have been US$20.

"We'll just have to pray that God will supply this need."

"But, *senhora,* it is due tomorrow!" this new Christian declared.

During the last two months my generous missionary husband had come up with what was lacking and other times he came up with "loans" which we would pay back. But we always needed to borrow again.

We decided we were depending upon ourselves too much and needed to allow God to supply our needs through other people. My husband said his empty pockets would be glad to rest awhile so other people could have a turn to be blessed by giving.

"Celina," I said into the phone, "let's pray right now on the phone. Our loving Father has promised not to leave us orphans. He delights in meeting our needs."

So, we prayed!

Right after the family had finished the evening meal, a missionary family from the state north of us stopped by on their way to Campinas. The missionary wife whispered, "Shirley, can we go into the bedroom for a moment?"

"Sure."

Inside the room, Karen told me that she had received a birthday card from her father and the Lord had impressed her to stop by and give something to the Children's Home.

She opened up the card, and you can guess

what was in it—a US$20 bill.

"I'm sorry I am late getting this to you."

"Oh, you are not late. You are right on time!"

We were both almost near tears as I told her how God used her to pay the phone rent. After they left that night, I made one of the happiest phone calls to Celina that a new Christian could receive. Keep your eyes on Jesus and He will help you walk on the water!

Our newest missionary at the time, Curt, was always encouraging us by pounding nails and repairing something around the home. But on several occasions, payment deadlines were right on us with no means to meet them when he and his wife would hand us something God impressed them to give. God is a great bookkeeper and makes it possible to fulfill the commandment, "Owe no man anything, except love."

Not Spent in Europe

Once, a church member called me to pick up a donation for the Children's Home which someone had left at her house.

After I arrived she explained, "Our neighbor has traveled to Europe, and before leaving he left this envelope for the home. You have never met him. He has never visited the home, but he has heard good things about your work with the street children."

It was a US$100 bill. It was more than enough to pay the pharmacy bill due that week!

Six Foot, Ten Inches of Obedience

One month a large financial responsibility was facing the Children's Home. The regular cake sales and special drives were all needed to meet the monthly expenses. This was a greater need than any idea we could come up with in our staff

THEY DESERVE A SECOND CHANCE

meeting.

About that time, Jim, my husband, received a phone call asking about the Children's Home. The caller was speaking English.

"My name is Anthony White," he offered, "and I am a professional basketball player with the Blue Life Team in Rio Claro. I heard about your work with street children in Araras and I would like to talk with you folks."

Anthony arrived with a box of canned goods for the home collected by the *Atletas de Cristo* (Athletes for Christ). He is a Baptist from Texas. He, his wife and two children had been in Brazil for several months and were touched by the assassinations of street children and the great need for a ministry to address this problem.

He visited the children at the home. As they all sat on the floor around him, he talked with them using the Portuguese phrases he had learned. However, when he gave his testimony he wanted to be sure his message got across to the children and asked me to interpret for him.

One little boy, Alex, asked, *"Porque ele e tao alto?"*

"God created Anthony that way—all six feet and ten inches," I replied in Portuguese.

"What did the boy ask you?" Tony questioned.

"Why are you so tall?" I smiled at him seated on the floor. "Help me talk to him," Tony said. "I want to answer that for him."

Anthony stood up and looked down on the little children seated on the floor. He began, "God created me extra tall so that I could play professional basketball and be invited to play on teams that travel all over the world. In every country, wherever I go, I look for boys and girls so I can tell them that Jesus loves them. I grew tall physically but I must also grow spiritually, just like you. It is important

THEY DESERVE A SECOND CHANCE

for you to have healthy bodies and to love God by knowing Jesus as your Savior."

What a role model for those children seated there! Most of the men in their families were addicts, criminals, or unemployed and illiterate. They beat and abused their neighbors, wives and children and the only religion they practiced was black magic and voodoo to put curses on their enemies.

Benefit Game

Anthony took a personal interest in the Children's Home and offered to arrange a benefit basketball game. He talked with the Brazilian Athletes for Christ and the Christian members of the Blue Life Team and asked them to play against All Star Players from various teams in Brazil.

It was to be a novelty for the city. If a sporting event were volleyball or the national sport of soccer, it would almost be guaranteed to be a success. At that time, not many people knew much about basketball, so advertisement was to prove important.

Good things started happening. The city sports arena was offered at no cost. Tickets were printed at no charge and many volunteers began selling pregame tickets. Local newspapers printed articles, the radio called us for live interviews and even a little television coverage was given. Friends from other churches offered to help us with the snack shop and prepared hundreds of *pasteis* (fried meat pies), *brigadeiros* (chocolate candy) and soft drinks. Local businesses donated nice sports gifts for door prizes. The competing teams did not charge for their services, and they showed up! We were ready to open the gates for game time.

And in they came. There was a better turn-out than anyone expected and the teams put on a great night of entertainment.

THEY DESERVE A SECOND CHANCE

The children from the Children's Home ate their fill of *pasteis* and *brigadeiros* and clapped and laughed at the tallest men they had ever seen in their lives. Best of all, they and others saw male role models giving their testimonies of salvation in Jesus Christ and giving away Bibles right along with other cherished prizes.

Remember the large financial responsibility I told you we were facing before all this happened? God used a tall young Texan, far from home, to supply a need in a little church in Brazil. The financial need was a tall order and God used a tall ambassador for Christ to bless our lives.

THEY DESERVE A SECOND CHANCE

CHAPTER SIXTEEN

TO JUDGE WISELY

The Children's Home had been operating for three years and 28 people were living in a three bedroom rented house. Dr. Durval, the juvenile judge, really seemed to believe in the work we were doing. The need in the city was overwhelming and, for the first time, a place was available locally where he could send street children who were living in life-threatening situations. But both the judge and we were frustrated that dozens of other children still had no place of refuge.

A phone call came one afternoon informing us of a request which had been passed on to the judge. The request involved taking our girls from the home and giving them to the Catholic nuns who were thinking about opening an orphanage for girls.

What some thought to be a great plan to alleviate our crowded conditions, was like a stab in our heart. Even though I had total confidence the nuns would provide the children with food and shelter just as we were doing, 1 felt another change would be too upsetting to the girls we had. My first reaction was to tell authorities this: There are hundreds of other little girls still out in the streets. Let them help those girls.

Our goal is to provide a safe home atmosphere for our children, and we work constantly with relatives and friends of these children to try to reintegrate them into family units. When we are successful in this goal, it is still difficult to release

THEY DESERVE A SECOND CHANCE

children we love. It is hard to send them into the unknown and often into many of the same conditions they were taken from.

To be uprooted from the home they have known for the past several years to be placed into an institution situation with strangers, was difficult for them to sift through. It would mean sisters would be separated from brothers and from their church family that had been so supportive of them during their rehabilitation. They had just begun to trust us. The girls would also need to change schools.

The church began to pray and fast. Pastor Eliseu and Isabel, the vice president of the home, and other representatives scheduled a meeting with the judge. At that meeting, Judge Durval informed the group that he had ordered the girls to be taken from the home and given to the nuns. But he turned to Pastor Eliseu and asked, "Exactly what do you want from me?"

Pastor Eliseu and Isabel, backed by many prayers of the saints on at least two continents, explained that we wanted to keep the girls we had at the home. They recognized the crowded conditions, but the home had plans to build as soon as possible. We also planned to open up other "family homes" to better care for the children.

He continued to explain that the girls were integrated into the church and were part of his flock. He believed many other little girls were in the street who needed someone to care for them.

Judge Durval decided he would continue to send boys to the home and, in the future, he would send the girls to the nuns. He also allowed the home to keep the boys and girls we already had.

What a victory to be able to keep our girls!

And since that decision, the judge has sent more little girls to our home as well as to the nuns.

We will face other problems in the future,

THEY DESERVE A SECOND CHANCE

but my eyes must not be on the storms. The boisterous winds stir the waves on the sea of life, and I know many children are out there struggling against torture and death. But I also know an outstretched arm is reaching out to them. There is a God who cares!

CHAPTER SEVENTEEN

LOVE AND ACCEPTANCE

"No way," the frail little child declared. "I'm not going to pray for my father and mother, not after what they did to me."

His was a common reaction among the new arrivals at the Children's Home when told during family devotions that the Bible teaches people to honor their mother and father and to pray for their salvation.

One of the most important needs, and one of the most difficult to convince the child to receive or give, is love and acceptance. This includes forgiveness. But somehow, as the children pray for the salvation of their families, a type of positive feeling starts growing in their hearts. Perhaps as they compare the good life they have in a Christian home with the old life they left behind, they begin to feel some type of love toward their parents. They realize their families are still struggling in that old life.

Detective Angels

One day we found 10-year-old Maria curled on her bed crying. When we asked her why, she tearfully whispered through her tears, "I want to see my *mamae.*"

"Your mama? Oh, we don't know where she is, honey." "I want to see my *mamae!*"

"Listen sweetheart, God is your Father. Talk to Him about it. If He thinks you really need to see your mother, He can find her and bring her here."

By this time other sad, little girls were around Maria's bed. When one cries, they all cry. But Maria stretched out on her bed and buried her head in her pillow and one by one the others climbed into their bunk beds in silence.

Silence. Would it be a healing silence? Had I gone too far? These little children were just learning to trust this Father God of the Bible. What if they think He doesn't come through and their faith takes a setback?

No, no. We can never be big enough for the task, but thankfully we don't have to be. We have to plant the seed of faith in these little ones and the Holy Spirit will take over from there.

The very next day there was a clap at the gate. A short woman with her hair twisted around the back of her head said, "I'm looking for my daughter, Maria." Kids ran everywhere announcing that Maria's mother had arrived. By the time Maria shyly sat next to her mother on the veranda, word had passed through the house to workers and volunteers that God had answered Maria's prayers.

This alcoholic mother who had run after her daughter with a butcher knife, was no threat at the moment. She was touched when she heard how much God loved little Maria. He loved her so much He had found a wayward mother and brought her to the door.

Coincidence? Every six or eight months, Maria cries to see her mother. Three times her mother has appeared the day after she prayed.

Four Years of Tears

Eight-year-old Cristiano cried one day to see his *mamae*. His story held another dimension. His mother had left him four years earlier when he was four years of age. Nobody knew where she

THEY DESERVE A SECOND CHANCE

was! We knew his father was an alcoholic and in jail.

Was this an impossible request? We pointed him to the hope he can find in the Lord. "Listen, Cristiano, we don't know where your mother is, but God knows. You can talk to Him about it and if He thinks you need to see your mother, He can find her and bring her to you."

He quietly climbed into his bunk bed to let his tears fall onto his pillow.

With all my dedication, I cannot really fill the void these mothers have left in their children. Cristiano's void did not even have a face for he couldn't remember what his mother looked like. But he knew I wasn't his mother and I had my limits. But God doesn't!

A few days later, Cristiano went off to school and a woman appeared at the gate. She was a tall, thin young woman with fair skin and long wavy hair. She was looking for her son called Cristiano.

"I should have been expecting you," I explained as I escorted her onto the veranda and into the living room. "God loves your little boy so much that He brought you here in response to your child's prayer."

It was tempting to think, "Where have you been these four Christmas holidays and four birthdays? You look strong. Don't you know what you have done to your child?" But I did not say these things.

We explained that Cristiano was in school and she could wait for him. We showed her around the home and showed her Cristiano's room which he shared with five more boys.

Later, Cristiano bounced into the room in his school uniform holding up his notebook. My husband, Jim, was sitting there and Cristiano showed him his notebook.

"Tio Pastor (uncle pastor), look at the happy

THEY DESERVE A SECOND CHANCE

face I got today!"

"*Muito bom,* Cristiano, very good. But we want to present you to someone visiting today."

Cristiano turned to the stranger sitting in a nearby chair. *"Boa tarde, senhora,"* he politely greeted and quickly turned back to Jim. "Look, I got another happy face."

The stranger sat stiffly in her chair, waiting.

We praised him and I pulled him toward me and put my arm around him, "Cristiano, this visitor is someone special. Do you remember your special prayer the other night?"

His expression was puzzled as he tried to remember. Then, he began sizing up the situation: "You mean ... *mamae"* "Yes dear, this is your mother."

He turned toward the woman and at the same moment they reached toward each other. He wrapped his slender arms around her neck and cried, *"Mamae!"*

He didn't ask where she had been the past Christmas holidays and birthdays. He just hugged the woman who finally provided a face to the image that had been erased from his little memory after four years of separation. Forgiveness. Happiness.

They weren't the only ones happy. Our whole household was rejoicing with them.

The two had a wonderful visit. The mother pulled off her watch and gave it to her son who didn't know how to tell time. She asked permission to take him across the street to a popcorn vendor.

"Sure, and you can walk around the *praca* (city square) here in front of the home and have a good visit."

She has never returned and he has not asked for her again. But that is one answer to prayer that he can always cherish. His mother's arms left him, but God, his Father, never, never will.

THEY DESERVE A SECOND CHANCE

Comin' To Get Me

Our ten-year-old Nelson is a special child with special needs. He attends a school for the mentally deficient and we are told that he will never be able to read or write. But in general he is a healthy child. He can feed himself and is learning to dress himself (if it doesn't matter how it is put together).

Psychiatrists haven't decided how much of his condition is trauma and how much can be done for him. Neighbors confirm his repeated story that he helped his mother drag and dump a man's body into a river. He says his father "chops up" like a butcher does a pig. He says he doesn't like pigs. Professionals aren't sure to what memories he might be referring.

He is improving. It has been a while since he has set something on fire or dumped a month's supply of beans into the dirt in the backyard. He is improving (or we are more alert) and he hasn't thrown anymore of our babies in buggies off the high porch and down the stairs and we haven't had to rescue any more two-year-olds from water where he has thrown them.

One day this special child declared dry-eyed, "I want to see my *mamae e papai.*" This is the first time a child has asked to see both parents.

If we tell him to pray to God, will he understand? We know that he loves to sing songs of the church and he sits quietly on the pew during the services. But what about prayer? We just know that God loves this child as much as the Marias and Cristianos of this world.

"Nelson, we don't know where your parents are, but God knows. Talk to Him about it and if He thinks you need to see your *mamae e papai,* He can find them and bring them to you."

His eyes held a blank stare and he quietly lay

THEY DESERVE A SECOND CHANCE

on his bottom bunk in a room full of other little boys—little ears and minds that may have been wondering the, same thing as 1.

That same week a couple came to the gate looking for their son, Nelson. The other children started running and calling for Nelson (you don't need an intercom system at *Lar Nova Vida).*

He proudly came out onto the veranda and hugged his parents and they sat and visited with many of the other little ones gathered around them.

"Son," his dad said, "I have arranged for a house. It is not very big. It's very simple, but it will be okay. In six weeks I'm coming to get you. We are going to be a family again!"

Soon volunteers and children were repeating what his dad had said. He was preparing a house for them and in six weeks he was coming to get him.

Two years later, Nelson still asks , "Are six weeks up yet?" "Yes, sweetheart, they are."

"Cause my daddy is preparing a place and he is coming to get me."

In a few days he has forgotten the answer and asks, "Have six weeks passed yet?"

"Yes, Nelson. I'm sorry but they have passed."

"Cause my daddy is preparing a house and he is coming to get me."

Praise God, we know one promise that won't be broken. Our Lord has gone to prepare a place for us and He is coming to get us.

We can make that promise to all of our children, Nelson included, and to any child on this globe, because our Heavenly Father is a promise keeper.

THEY DESERVE A SECOND CHANCE

CHAPTER EIGHTEEN

THE GUILTY BRIDE REVEALS HER SECRET

"When you kill a street boy," a public prosecutor in Brazil told a reporter, "you take out one of the worst ones, and you also give an example to the others. You are exercising social control through fear."

A stirring report in a Christian magazine declared that over a period of five years, nearly 1,500 murders of children have been recorded in 16 Brazilian states. Bodies of children have mysteriously turned up floating in the open sewer. Others were found shot in public squares as they slept during the night. Some were discovered stabbed. Others simply vanished.

These are street children. They beg and steal in the streets or they die. The street kids (boys and girls) graduate quickly from minor thefts and begging to prostitution and drug running for adults. A growing number of AIDS victims are found among these children.

These helpless lambs have come from cramped, makeshift slum villages where they have lived in sub-human conditions, with little food, little running water and little sanitation. Many of them don't know their fathers. Some of their fathers have even been murdered. Their mothers are sometimes addicted to drugs or alcohol and may sleep with one man, then another. They don't want her kids around.

But who is killing these defenseless children? Most signs point to paramilitary ex-policemen,

THEY DESERVE A SECOND CHANCE

hired by businessmen. The children themselves say the police make them steal, then they take the money and loot from frightened kids. Having taken advantage of them already, they order the children to steal more, or die.

The citizens—shopkeepers and the public—fear these children so they have chosen guards and policemen to act as executioners. They have lost hope that anything can help the children. They doubt these can ever be anything but vagabonds or drug runners.

The children also have lost hope. The very authority figures who should be nurturing and protecting them are using them and abusing them. In some cases they are killing them.

Is there hope? That depends. The Church, the Bride, holds the hope in the truth of the gospel. She must identify with the needs of her community and identify with solutions found in the power of a sovereign God.

If the Church is silent, then, to a hurting world, God is silent. If the Bride is detached and uninformed, then God is far away and ignorant of the peril of those drowning in this tempestuous sea of misery. She must not hold the hope of the gospel as if it were a secret for only a few.

Before we brought the first street child into our own home and then opened *Lar Nova Vida*, our heart cried out to identify, to rescue, to love, to hold, to protect those little ones. We longed to declare, "Yes, God is powerful. Yes, He is sovereign. Yes, He is near and knows their peril. Yes, there is hope in Jesus!"

It still hurts but not quite as much. We are seeing a difference as we see God's power reach out to these little ones.

How can a person or church start? Look into the eyes of Jesus, take His outstretched hand and

THEY DESERVE A SECOND CHANCE

just start walking on the water. In this book, I have shared with you how we began our walk, but you must look at your community and determine your walk.

How long will we walk? Does it matter?

In one day's time, I have been in the luxurious home of a state political leader, praying over a complicated need, and then ended up in the most grimy, squalid corner of our city carrying out a maggot infested mattress from the hut of a paralyzed woman. Although her notorious husband cursed and terrorized and ran out the curious neighbors, I was able to empty slop jars, scrape out molded food, pray for the woman and bring her a mattress and blanket. I have claimed the words of a familiar hymn:

> *If Jesus goes with me I'll go,*
> *Anywhere!*
> *Tis heaven to me, where'er I may be,*
> *If He is there.*
> *I count it a privilege here.*
> His cross to bear.
> *If Jesus goes with me I'll go,*
> *Anywhere!*

Dr. Durval, the juvenile judge in Araras, shared this challenge one day: "The world's children have no frontiers. We are all responsible for the suffering children of the world, no matter where they are. We must begin by desiring for all children what we can give to our own children."

The mayor's wife and director of the Department of Human Services made this statement concerning our church: "Our city has gained by the involvement of the *Igreja Batista Livre* with the street children of our city. We were seeking a way to reach this great need. The *Lar Nova Vida* has provided that necessary link between those

THEY DESERVE A SECOND CHANCE

of us who have and want to give, and those who do not have and need to receive. We have all gained. Our city and our children."

Oh, yes, *Dona Olga*, we have all gained! But most of all, the children have gained hope and salvation in a loving Father.

They are free to be children. Free to play and dream while they allow others to care for them.

Christ gave His life for His Bride, the Church. She must not be guilty of holding in secret what the world needs. When she reaches out to children who are victims of violence and poverty and gives them life and hope, she has gained. And God has been glorified!

Jesus loves the little children—the homeless on American city streets and on the cobblestone *ruas* (streets) of Brazil as well as those on jungle paths—ALL THE CHILDREN OF THE WORLD!

Remember, He told Peter to "feed my lambs." That is our challenge, too!

Made in the USA
Columbia, SC
02 June 2022